Teaching Units for the
Giant Book of
Theme Patterns

by Jean Stangl

Illustration and Design by
Walt Shelly

Fearon Teacher Aids
Simon & Schuster Education Group

Editorial Director: Virginia L. Murphy
Editor: Carol Williams
Copyeditor: Kristin Eclov
Illustration and Design: Walt Shelly

ISBN 0-86653-966-2

Printed in the United States of America
1. 9 8 7 6 5 4 3 2

Contents

Introduction

Teaching Units is a companion book to *The Giant Book of Theme Patterns*. This valuable resource provides numerous innovative ways to use the 400 plus theme patterns in the classroom.

Teaching Units offers complete directions and specific guidelines for projects in all subject areas.

The projects will give your students many opportunities to trace, cut, color, glue, and paint while reinforcing useful skills and important information in science, math, social studies, and language arts. And, the possibilities for holiday projects are endless with the large selection of festive patterns and teaching ideas. Some projects are best done individually, some in small groups, and some as a whole class.

The many options presented are only a few of the possible use for the theme patterns provided. Use your creative resources and encourage students to expand upon the ideas and suggestions. If young children have access to a variety of creative art materials and boxes of "good junk," they will use these patterns and their imaginations to create surprising and satisfying projects.

Language Arts

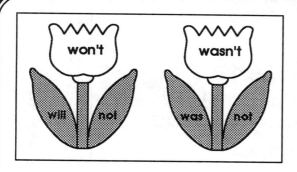

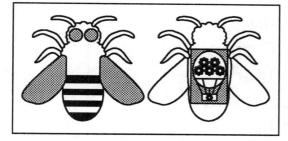

Words and Letters

Wild Animal Alphabet Book
Pairs on a Pear Tree
Antonym Tree
Compound People
Spell That, Please
Grow a Tulip Garden
Rhyme Time
What's Bugging You?
Beehive Box
Color Connection
Who Can Find It?

Wild Animal Alphabet Book
Patterns: Wild Animal patterns, pages 91-128

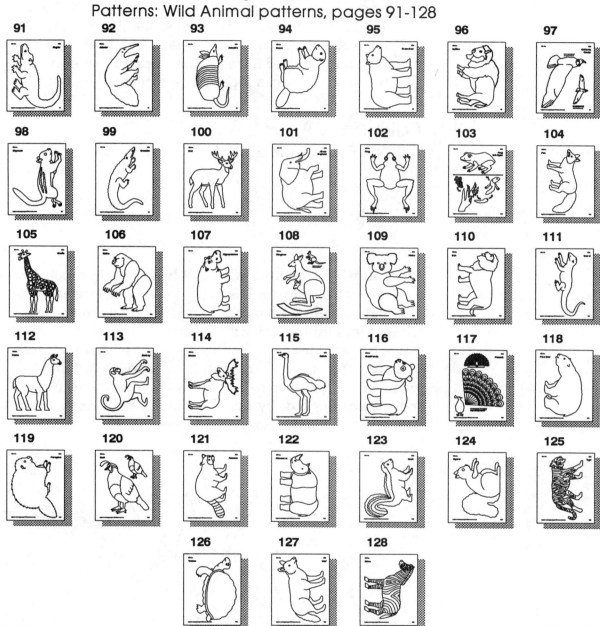

Share David McPhail's *Animals from A to Z* (New York: Scholastic, 1988) with your students. Assign each student a letter of the alphabet and give each student an animal pattern to represent that letter (A=alligator, B=buffalo, and so on). For letters that do not have an animal pattern, use some creative license. For example, to represent the letter U, use an upside-down monkey. Invite students to color and cut out their animals. Encourage students to glue their animals on 8 1/2" x 11" sheets of construction paper. Help children write the appropriate uppercase and lowercase letters and spell the animals' names. Combine all the pages together in a class alphabet book.

Pairs on a Pear Tree

Pattern: Pear, page 251

251

Plant a dried tree limb with full branches in a pot of wet sand. Give each student a copy of the pear pattern. Invite each student to trace and cut a yellow pear and a green pear from construction paper. Challenge children to write pairs of homonyms (words that sound alike, but are spelled differently) on the pears. Punch a hole in the top of each pear shape. Help children connect the matching pears with yarn. Invite children to loop the yarn over a tree branch so the homonym pairs hang side by side. Encourage students to take the pears from the tree and use both words in a sentence.

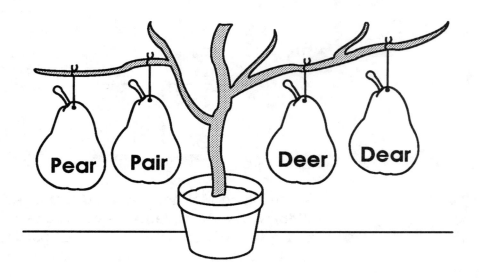

Antonym Tree

Patterns: Apple, page 249; Orange, page 248

249   **248**

Plant a dried tree limb with full branches in a pot of wet sand. Give each student a copy of the apple and orange patterns. Invite each student to trace and cut an orange from orange construction paper and an apple from red or green construction paper. Challenge children to write antonyms (opposites) on each pair of orange or apple shapes. Punch a hole in the top of each piece of fruit. Help the children connect the opposite pairs with yarn. Invite children to loop the yarn over a tree branch so the fruit pairs hang side by side.

Compound People

Pattern: Gingerbread Person, page 312

312

Make several cardboard gingerbread person patterns. Invite children to trace and cut out gingerbread people from brown construction paper. Write a compound word (cupcake, keyboard, breakfast, fingernail, yardstick, drumstick, nightgown) across the body of each gingerbread person. Laminate or cover each gingerbread person with clear adhesive-backed paper. Then cut the gingerbread people in half separating the compound words at the logical breaks. Make each cut unique using zigzag and curving lines. Invite children to play a game with a partner by matching the gingerbread halves to make compound words.

Spell That, Please
Patterns: Any patterns

Give each student a pattern to color and cut out. Invite students to mount the colored patterns on construction paper. Collect the patterns and write the names of the objects on the backsides. Place the cutouts in a paper bag at the language center. Invite students to work in pairs to practice spelling the words on the patterns. Encourage one student to hold a card and call out the word while the other partner spells the word. Encourage partners to switch roles so both receive spelling practice.

Grow a Tulip Garden
Pattern: Tulip, page 17

Write a list of contractions on the chalkboard. Beside the contractions, write the two words that make up the contraction (won't = will not). Give each student a tulip pattern. Invite students to trace and cut the two leaves from green and the tulip buds from pink, purple, or red construction paper. Have the children color the stem patterns green and glue each to an 8 1/2" x 11" sheet of blue construction paper. Encourage each student to neatly write a contraction on the tulip bud and the two words that make up the contraction on each leaf. Place all the stems in a stack and the tulip buds and leaves in a bag at the language center. Invite the children to match the tulip buds with the correct leaves. Arrange the tulips on the stems to create a garden of contractions.

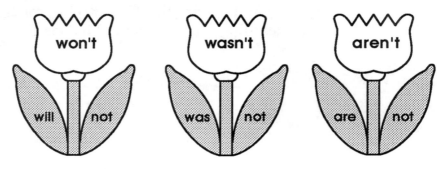

Rhyme Time

Pattern: Snail, page 184

184

Give each student a snail pattern. Invite children to color and cut out the snails. Challenge children to turn the snails over and write lists of words that rhyme with the word *snail* (there are over 50).

What's Bugging You?

Patterns: Grasshopper, page 177; Ladybug, page 178; Butterfly, page 180; Ant, page 182; Fly, page 183

177 **178** **180** **182** **183**

    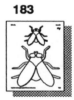

Give each student a bug pattern. Encourage each student to write or dictate a sentence or two on the bug describing his or her feelings about a problem. Help children realize that others often feel the same as they do. Encourage students to share their thoughts. Brainstorm ideas for workable solutions.

Beehive Box

Pattern: Hive and Honeybee, page 179

179

Enlarge the bee pattern and reproduce one for each child. Invite children to color and cut out their bees. Encourage half of the children to find magazine pictures that begin with the letter B and glue them to the back of their bee pictures. Invite the other half of the children to glue magazine pictures that do not start with the letter B on the backs of their bee pictures. Cut out and tape the beehive pattern to the side of a shoebox. Give each child an opportunity to tell what the picture is on the back of his or her bee. Then have the class decide if that bee belongs in the beehive (only words that begin with the letter B belong in the hive). If the word belongs in the hive, invite the child to come up and put it in. Try the activity again using other patterns and letters.

Color Connection

Patterns: Strawberry, page 255; Lemon, page 249; Blueberry, page 255; Lettuce, page 263; Bread, page 273; Cantaloupe, page 259; Potato, page 268; Grapes, page 253

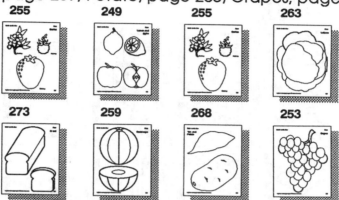

Cut a large circle from tagboard and divide it into eight equal pie shapes to make a color wheel. Write a color word in each section (red, yellow, blue, green, white, orange, brown, purple). Attach a spinner cut from tagboard to the center of the wheel using a paper fastener. Color the food patterns the appropriate colors to match the color words on the wheel. Cut the patterns out. Invite children to take turns spinning the wheel and finding a fruit pattern that matches the color word.

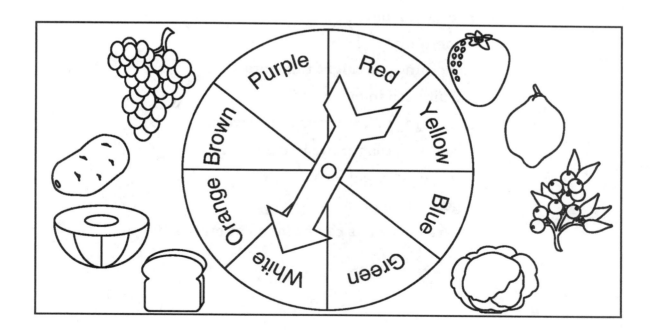

Who Can Find It?

Patterns: Lion, page 110; Scottie, page 140; Bus, page 238; Oak Leaf, page 1; Apple, page 249; Mitten, page 14; Rose, page 19; Star, page 49; Saw, page 287; Rocking Chair, page 227; Bed, page 221

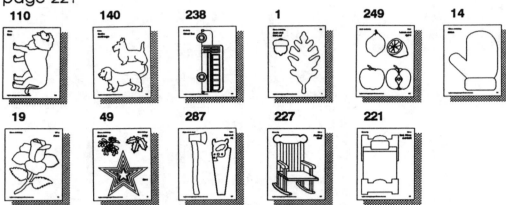

This is a great vocabulary development exercise for young children and second-language learners. Invite children to help you color and cut out the patterns. Mount each shape on an 8 1/2" x 11" piece of construction paper. Lay the pictures out on the floor of your classroom. Invite two children at a time to stand beside the group of pictures. Call out a clue and invite children to race each other to find the correct picture. Clues might include:

a large animal

something you ride in

something you might rake into a pile

a fruit used to make a pie

something to keep your hands warm

something that grows in a garden

a tool used to cut wood

a good place to sit

where most of us can be found at midnight

Literature

The Three Little Pigs
The Three Billy Goats Gruff
Goldilocks and the Three Bears
The Little Red Hen
Brown Bear, Brown Bear
Humpty Dumpty
Gingham Dog and Calico Cat
The Ugly Duckling
Giant Story Cube
Old MacDonald Had a Farm

The Three Little Pigs

Patterns: Three Pigs, page 297; Pigs' Houses, page 298; Wolf, page 127

297   **298** 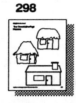 **127**

Read or tell the story of *The Three Little Pigs* to your students. Give each child the story-figure patterns. Encourage children to color both sides of the pig and wolf figures and then cut them out. Invite children to cut out the three houses and glue pieces of straw on both sides of one house, some sticks on another house, and some construction-paper bricks on the third house. Punch a hole in the top of each figure. Help each child hang the figures with yarn from a clothes hanger to make a story mobile. Children might also enjoy hearing *The True Story of the 3 Little Pigs* by Jon Scieszka (New York: Viking, 1989). This story is the wolf's account of these well-known events.

The Three Billy Goats Gruff

Patterns: Billy Goats, page 301; Troll, page 302

301  **302**

Read or tell the story of *The Three Billy Goats Gruff* to your students. Color and cut out each story-figure pattern. Make a bridge from construction paper. Mount a piece of sandpaper on the back of each figure. Drape a piece of flannel or felt over an easel. Invite children to use the story figures to retell the story as they place the characters on the flannel board.

Goldilocks and the Three Bears

Patterns: Goldilocks, page 299; Three Bears, page 300

Read or tell the story of *Goldilocks and the Three Bears* to your students. Divide children into groups of four and give each group the story-character patterns. Invite each group to cooperatively decide which group member will be which character. Have each child color and cut out his or her story character. Help children mount their characters on popsicle sticks to make stick puppets. While holding their stick puppets, invite children to take on the roles of their characters as they act out the story. Encourage children to collect other props they may need, such as bowls, spoons, chairs, and so on.

The Little Red Hen

Patterns: Hen and Chicks, page 166; Duck, page 168; Cat, page 129; Puppy, page 139

Read or tell the story of *The Little Red Hen* to your students. Give each child a set of story characters to color and cut out. Invite children to glue each character on the bottom flap of a lunch bag to make paper-bag puppets. Encourage children to make a puppet stage by cutting a window out of a large appliance box. Invite children to use their paper-bag puppets to retell the story.

Brown Bear, Brown Bear

Patterns: Brown Bear, page 95; Blue Jay, page 173; Duck, page 168; Mare, page 163; Frog, page 102; Cat, page 129; Puppy, page 139; Ewe, page 164; Fish, page 132

Read the story *Brown Bear, Brown Bear What Do You See?* by Bill Martin, Jr. (New York: Holt, Rinehart and Winston, 1983). Give each child a copy of the story-character patterns. Invite children to color the figures appropriately and cut them out. Help children glue the characters on separate sheets of construction paper. Punch two holes through the left side of the pages and tie yarn through the holes to hold the books together. Encourage students to retell the story using their wordless books.

Humpty Dumpty

Pattern: Eggs (Easter Eggs), page 83

Recite "Humpty Dumpty" together as a class. Give each student three egg patterns exactly the same size and three sheets of construction paper. Invite children to use the egg patterns to recreate three scenes from the "Humpty Dumpty" nursery rhyme. For example, in the first scene students could draw a wall and glue Humpty Dumpty on top of it. In the second scene, students could depict the "great fall" by once again drawing the wall and gluing the egg falling through the air. For the final scene, students could cut the egg into several pieces and glue them at the base of the wall.

Gingham Dog and Calico Cat

Patterns: Puppy, page 139; Cat, page 129

139 **129**

Read Eugene Field's poem "The Duel" to your students. Give each student a copy of the puppy and cat patterns. Invite children to trace and cut the puppy pattern from graph paper. Show children how to make a gingham design by coloring alternate squares on the graph paper. Invite children to trace and cut the cat pattern from white construction paper. Show children how to draw patchwork calico designs on the cat. Encourage students to add facial features to their gingham dogs and calico cats using construction-paper scraps. Invite children to recreate that famous spat as you read the poem again.

The Ugly Duckling

Patterns: Duckling, page 168; Swan, page 170

168 **170**

Read or tell the story of *The Ugly Duckling* by Hans Christian Andersen. Give each student a copy of the duckling and swan patterns. Invite students to make double-sided stick puppets with the ugly duckling on one side and the beautiful swan on the other. Invite students to use their stick puppets to retell the story.

Giant Story Cube

Patterns: Jack and the Beanstalk, page 304; Giant, page 303; Little Red Riding Hood, page 305; Big Bad Wolf, page 306; Tortoise, page 126; Rabbit, page 160; Fox, page 104; Grapes, page 253; Prince, page 309; Princess, page 308; Dragon, page 313; Gingerbread Person, page 312; Crocodile, page 99

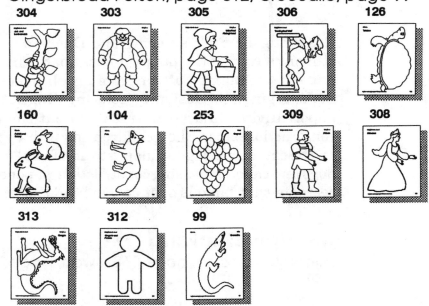

Cover several large, square cardboard boxes with butcher paper. Give a covered box to each group of six students. Give a copy of the story-character patterns to each group. Invite children to color and cut out the story characters and glue them to the six sides of the boxes. Each box panel should represent one of the following stories or fables:

Jack and the Beanstalk

Little Red Riding Hood

The Tortoise and the Hare

The Fox and the Grapes

The Gingerbread Man

any fairy tale

When the boxes are complete, encourage students to roll the huge dice and tell or act out the stories that land on top.

Old MacDonald Had a Farm

Patterns: Cow, page 161; Mare, page, 163; Ewe, page 164; Sow, page 165; Hen, page 166; Rooster, page 167; Duck, page 168

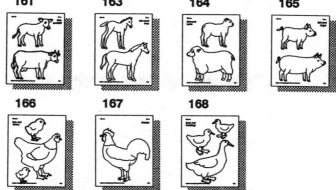

Give each student a character pattern. Invite students to color and cut out their animals and glue them to wooden paint stirring sticks, popsicle sticks, or tongue depressors. Invite children with the same characters to form a group and decide on a sound for their animal. Sing "Old MacDonald Had a Farm" together as a class. Encourage each group to make their animal sound at the appropriate places in the song.

Creative Writing

Alligators All Around
Goldfish Gossip
Three-Character Story
Dinner Guest
Shape Stories
Westward Ho!
Greeting Cards
Dinosaur Riddles
What If I Lived with a Dinosaur?
Perfect Pets

Alligators All Around

Pattern: Ducklings, page 168

168

Read the alphabet book *Alligators All Around* by Maurice Sendak (New York: Harper & Row, 1962) to your students. Use the alphabetical pattern of alliterative phrases to make your own classroom alphabet book. Give each student a copy of the duckling patterns and assign each student a letter of the alphabet. Invite each student to think of an alliterative phrase (using the assigned alphabet letter) that describes an action. Encourage students to color and cut out the ducklings and glue them on sheets of construction paper. Invite students to add details to the ducks so they appear to be performing the actions in the alliterative phrase. For example, the ducklings could be creating cartoons, fixing fences, or picking peaches. Have students write the phrases below the pictures. Assemble the pictures in alphabetical order to make a class book.

Goldfish Gossip

Pattern: Fish, page 132

132

If possible, provide a small aquarium or fishbowl in your classroom and fill it with goldfish. Invite students to observe the fish and imagine what they might be thinking or saying to each other. Encourage students to cut out and glue the fish patterns to sheets of construction paper. Have children draw dialogue bubbles above the fish and write or dictate fish phrases and goldfish gossip.

Three-Character Story

Patterns: Any patterns

Give each student a different pattern. Divide students into groups of three. Encourage children to color and cut out their characters. Invite children to glue the characters on popsicle sticks or empty paper-towel tubes to make stick puppets. Encourage group members to work cooperatively to create a story featuring their three characters. Give each group an opportunity to act out their story for the class.

Dinner Guest

Pattern: Table and Chairs, page 229

229

Give each child a copy of the table and chair patterns. Invite each child to color and cut out the patterns and glue them on one side of a 12" x 18" sheet of construction paper. Encourage children to draw themselves sitting in one chair and a picture of the person they would most like to have dinner with in the other chair. Encourage children to write or dictate paragraphs that describe their dinner guests and explain why they chose this person as their dinner companion. Glue the descriptions on the other side of the construction paper.

Shape Stories

Fishbowl, page 133; Stop Sign, page 190; Postal Truck, page 200;
Pineapple, page 257; Watermelon, page 258; Basketball,
page 296

133 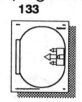 **190**  **200** 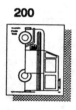 **257** 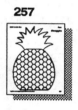 **258**  **296**

Invite each child to select one pattern. Help the children trace and cut
two pattern shapes from construction paper to make the front and back
covers of each shape booklet. Help the children cut several sheets of
lined paper in the same shape. Staple the pages between the covers.
Encourage children to brainstorm a list of words that begin with the
same letter as the item pictured on their shape booklets. Challenge the
children to write stories using the shapes of their booklets as the main
emphasis. Encourage students to use as many words from their lists
as possible in their stories.

Westward Ho!

Patterns: Covered Wagon, page 208; Oxen, page 209

208 **209**

Give each child a covered wagon pattern and the two oxen. Invite children to color and cut out the patterns. Encourage children to glue the
team of oxen and the covered wagon to a large sheet of paper. Help the
children loop brown yarn between the two animals and then to the
wagon, then glue the yarn in place. Invite children to draw mountains,
rivers, and trees to add details to their pictures. Challenge children to
write an adventure story about their travels.

Greeting Cards

Patterns: Sunflower, page 8; Pinecone, page 4; Daisy, page 16, Tulip, page 17; Water Lily on Pad, page 18; Rose, page 19; Rainbow, page 22; Shamrock, page 79; Firecracker, page 89; Hatching Chick, page 84; Poodle, page 138

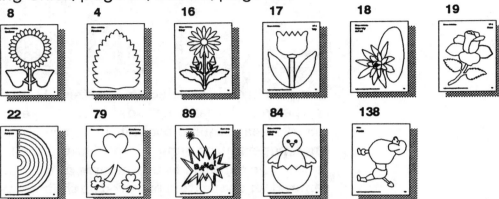

Invite children to select a pattern. Have each child trace the pattern onto a piece of construction paper. Help the children cut out and glue the shapes onto folded pieces of construction paper to make cards. Encourage children to decorate their greeting cards and write or dictate original messages or poems inside.

Dinosaur Riddles

Patterns: Brontosaurus, page 185; Stegosaurus, page 186; Triceratops, page 187; Tyrannosaurus, page 188

185 **186** **187** **188**

  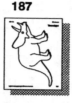 

Share some riddles with your students from *Tyrannosaurus Wrecks* by Noelle Sterne (New York: Thomas Y. Crowell, 1979). Encourage students to write their own riddles and illustrate them using the dinosaur patterns.

What If I Lived with a Dinosaur?

Patterns: Brontosaurus, page 185; Stegosaurus, page 186; Triceratops, page 187; Tyrannosaurus, page 188

185 **186** **187** **188**

Read *Danny and the Dinosaur* by Syd Hoff (New York: Harper & Row, 1958) to your students. In the story, Danny and the dinosaur go to a ball game together, share ice cream, and go to the zoo. Of course, they make quite a spectacle and the day turns out to be like no other. Invite each child to choose a dinosaur and think of some fun activities he or she might like to do with this new friend. Encourage students to write short stories about their adventures. Invite children to illustrate the crazy antics using the dinosaur patterns.

Perfect Pets

Patterns: Cat, page 129, Cockatoo, page 130; Collie, page 131; Fish, page 132; Gerbil, page 134; German Shepherd, page 135; Kitten, page 136; Mouse, page 137; Poodle, page 138; Puppy, page 139; Scottie and Beagle, page 140; Rabbit, page 160

Invite each student to select a pattern that represents the perfect pet. Invite children to glue the pet patterns to tagboard and cut them out. Encourage children to color their pets and add cardboard stands to the backs so their pets will stand upright as well. Challenge the children to write persuasive paragraphs explaining why their animals are the most perfect pets. Display the pets and paragraphs around the classroom.

Math

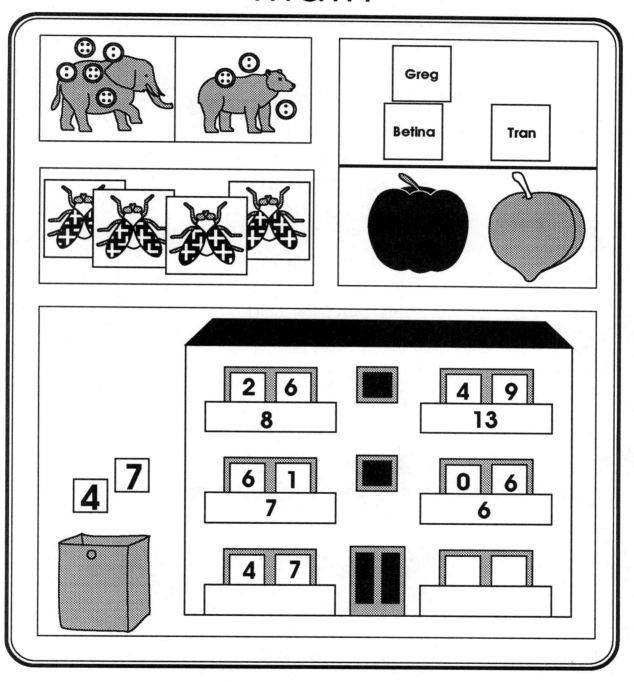

Sorting and Graphing

Search and Sort
Shape Sizes
Fav-o-graph
People Graph
Fish Fry
What Else Belongs?
Almost Identical
Fly Swatter Sort

Search and Sort

Patterns: Sun, page 25; Star, page 49; Bell, page 50; Eggs (Easter Eggs), page 83; Shamrock, page 79; Heart, page 75; Sand Dollar, page 157; Seashells, page 159; Berries, page 255

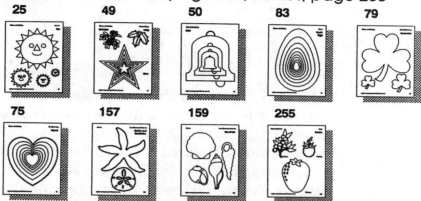

Give each child several small patterns to color and cut out. Laminate the patterns or cover them with clear adhesive-backed paper. Place all the patterns in a bag or box at the math learning center. Invite children to empty the bag or box and sort the patterns by color, size, or shape. Encourage students to create patterns using the shapes , such as bell, bell, sun, bell bell, heart, and so on.

Shape Sizes

Patterns: Hearts, page 75; Stars, page 49; Eggs (Easter Eggs), page 83; Bells, page 50

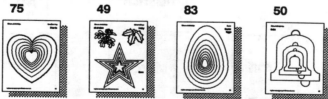

Trace and cut each size heart, star, egg, and bell from tagboard to make sturdy patterns for children. Invite each child to choose one shape to trace and cut out all the sizes from construction paper. Challenge children to place the shapes in order from smallest to largest or largest to smallest. Punch a hole in both ends of each shape and invite children to string the shapes on a piece of yarn in descending or ascending order.

Fav-o-graph

Patterns: Apple, page 249; Peach, page 250; Pear, page 251;
Grapes, page 253; Banana, page 254

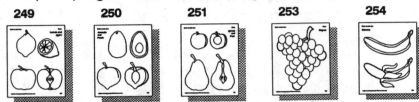

Color and cut out each fruit pattern. Place the pictures along the
bottom of a posterboard, bulletin board, or chalkboard. Give each child
a small square of construction paper. Ask children to write their names
on the squares. In turn, invite each child to tape the square above his
or her favorite fruit so the squares form a vertical line above the
pictures. When the graph is complete, analyze the results by asking
questions, such as "How many children chose a peach as their favorite
fruit?" "Which fruit is least liked?" "How many more children chose
grapes than bananas?" Try making another graph using favorite
animals or favorite seasons of the year.

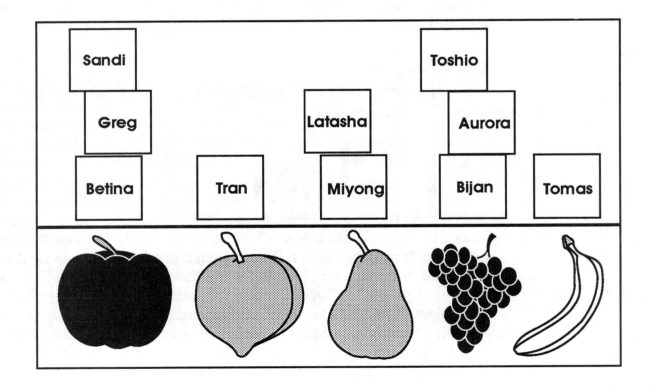

People Graph

Patterns: Bicycle, page 193; School Bus, page 238; Car, page 195; Pedestrian Sign, page 189

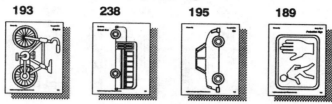

Ask children how they got to school today. Give each child a pattern to represent that means of transportation. Encourage children to color and cut out the patterns. Invite all children who have a car pattern to stand in one line, all children who walked to school to stand in another line, and so on until four parallel lines are formed. Challenge children to analyze the data represented by this people graph.

Fish Fry

Patterns: Saltwater Fish, page 152

Give each child a copy of the saltwater fish patterns. Invite children to color the fish solid colors and then cut them out. Mount each fish on a 5" x 7" piece of construction paper. Use the same color of construction paper to mount all of the fish. Invite children to play a matching game using the fish cards. Turn all the fish cards face down. Invite each child in turn to flip over two cards. If the child can identify a similarity between the two fish, he or she can keep the "catch." For example, the two fish may be the same color or the same shape. If a match is made, the player continues. If the two fish do not match, the cards are turned back over. The player with the most fish at the end of the game is the winner.

What Else Belongs?

Patterns: Roller Skate, page 202; Helicopter, page 197; Shovel, page 284; Toothbrush, page 243

202   **197**    **284** 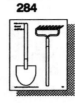   **243**

Display a picture of a roller skate. Ask a child to name another item that would belong in the same category as a roller skate and tell why. For example, the child may say that a wagon belongs in the category because both a roller skate and a wagon have wheels. Then invite other children to add to the category by naming other items that have wheels. Display other pictures, such as a helicopter, shovel, or toothbrush and challenge students to add items to the categories. Glue each picture on a separate piece of tagboard. Invite children to draw or cut pictures from magazines to add to each category. Write the rule for each group on the posterboard.

Almost Identical

Pattern: Mask, page 39

39

Give each child two copies of the mask pattern. Invite children to color both masks so they are identical except for one part. For example, a child may color the nose on one mask blue and the nose on the other mask purple. Invite each child to show both of his or her masks to the class and challenge others to find the differences.

Fly Swatter Sort

Pattern: Fly, page 183

183

Trace the small fly pattern four times on a sheet of paper. Reproduce the sheet and give one to each child. Invite children to color all four of their flies so they look identical. Have children include some distinguishing characteristics on all four pictures (red eyes, one green wing, or purple legs). Invite children to cut around the flies and mount them on 4" squares of white construction paper. In groups of four, invite children to play "Fly Swatter Sort." Combine the fly cards from all four children and deal four cards to each student. Invite one player to lay down a card from his or her hand. The first player who swats it with a hand can take the card and discard another card. The discarded card can then be swatted by another player who then can take the card and discard. Play continues until one player has a set of identical fly pictures.

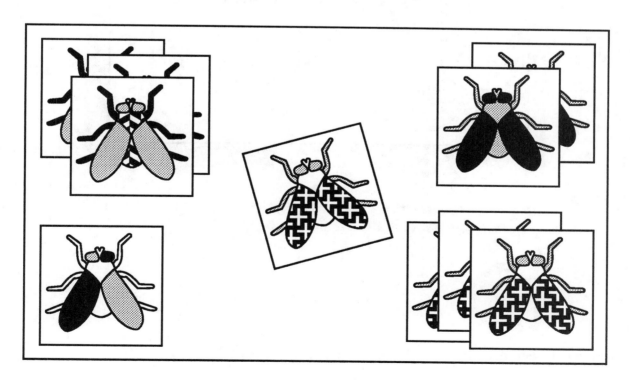

Numbers and Operations

Dot to Dot
More Than, Less Than
Number Hop
Equal Share
Dial-a-Number
Nutty Numbers
Math Puzzlers
Counting Cards
Apartment Addition

Dot to Dot
Patterns: Any pattern

Place a sheet of drawing paper over any pattern. Make small dots around the outline of the pattern. Number the dots in the order they should be connected. Number by ones, twos, fives, or tens. Reproduce the dotted drawing and give a copy to each student. Challenge students to connect the dots in order to discover the hidden picture. Invite students to color the completed outlines.

More Than, Less Than
Patterns: African Elephant, page 101; Brown Bear, page 95

Give each student a copy of the elephant and bear patterns. Invite students to color and cut out the animal shapes. Have each student draw a heavy line to divide a 12" x 18" sheet of construction paper in half. Have students glue the elephants on one side and the bears on the other. Give each student a supply of counters, such as beads, toothpicks, beans, or buttons. Instruct students to place five counters on the elephant and three counters on the bear. Ask students to identify which side has more or less. Ask students to add or remove enough counters to make both sides equal. Continue giving directions for creating unequal sides and ask students to identify which side has more or less. Encourage students to write number sentences to represent their concrete examples.

Number Hop
Pattern: Frog, page 102

102

Give each student a frog pattern. Encourage students to color the frogs and cut them out. Using adding machine tape, make a number line from 0-20 for each group of four students. Space each number on the line 6" apart. Duplicate some task card questions for each group. Invite students to use their frogs to hop the number line and calculate the answers. Questions could include, "If the frog starts on 12 and jumps three marks to the right, what number will it land on?" "If the frog begins on an even number and jumps three spaces in either direction, will it land on an even or odd number?" "If the frog begins on 17 and wants to end on 3, how many spaces will it need to jump and in which direction?"

Equal Share
Patterns: Corn, page 5; Pumpkin, page 6; Pineapple, page 257; A Dozen Eggs in a Carton, page 269

5   **6**   **257**   **269**

Read *Gator Pie* by Louise Mathews (New York: Dodd, Mead, 1979) to your students. In the story, two alligators decide to divide a pie among their friends. Give each pair of students a corncob, pumpkin, pineapple, and carton of eggs pattern. Challenge students to divide the patterns in half so that both partners have an equal share. Point out that dividing the items on the line of symmetry makes identical halves.

Dial-a-Number

Pattern: Telephone, page 230

230

Give each child a copy of the telephone pattern. Invite children to write their own phone numbers at the bottom of the pages. Invite each child to read his or her telephone number while other classmates "dial" it on their own telephones. Discuss the emergency number 911 and help children practice dialing it as well.

Nutty Numbers

Pattern: Nuts (Almond, Brazil Nut, Peanut, and Walnut), page 252

252

Give each child a copy of the nut patterns. Assign each child four numbers. Give the first child numbers 1-4, the second child 5-8, the third child 9-12, and so on so that no two children have the same numbers. Have each child write one number on each of the four whole nuts. Invite children to cut the nuts out and place them on their desk tops. Call out number sentences, patterns, and groupings. Invite children with the targeted numbers to stand and call out their numbers. For example, if you call out the number pattern 8, 12, 16, ___, the child with the number 20 written on one of his or her nuts would stand. Ask for all children with numbers less than 20 to stand. Have each child read off his or her number(s) in order beginning with the child who has number 1. Give mental math problems, such as 3 plus 5 minus 2equals___. Invite the child with the correct answer to stand. Fire off a variety of instructions at a quick pace so all children are involved and participating equally.

Math Puzzlers
Patterns: Any pattern

Give each child a pattern. Invite children to use rulers to draw lines dividing the patterns into 8 to 10 pieces. Have children write math problems on some edges of the puzzle pieces and answers to the problems on the edges of the puzzle pieces that connect to them. Children can color the pictures being careful not to color over the math problems making them unreadable. Laminate the puzzles or cover them with clear adhesive-backed paper. Invite children to cut the puzzles apart. Put each puzzle in a separate zip lock baggie. Challenge children to select puzzles and try to put them together using the math problems and answers as clues.

Counting Cards
Patterns: Hearts, page 75; Stars, page 49; Eggs (Easter Eggs), page 83; Bells, page 50

75   **49**   **83**   **50**

Trace several small patterns on a sheet of drawing paper. Reproduce the sheet for each student. Invite students to color and cut out the shapes. Give each group of three students eleven 8 1/2" x 11" pieces of construction paper. Have each group make a set of counting cards by gluing one pattern on one card, two patterns on another card, three on a third card, and so on. Help children write the numeral and the number word on the cards from "zero" to "ten."

Apartment Addition

Pattern: Apartment, page 220

220

Give each child a copy of the apartment pattern. Give each pair of children ten 1" squares of construction paper and a paper bag. Have children write the numbers 0-9 on the squares and place them in the paper bag. Instruct children to work in pairs taking turns reaching in the bag and pulling out a number. Have children write each number in one of the pairs of apartment windows. Have children return the number to the bag after each draw and pull out another one until all six pairs of apartment windows have a number written in them. Challenge children to add the numbers in each pair of windows and write the answers in the window boxes below.

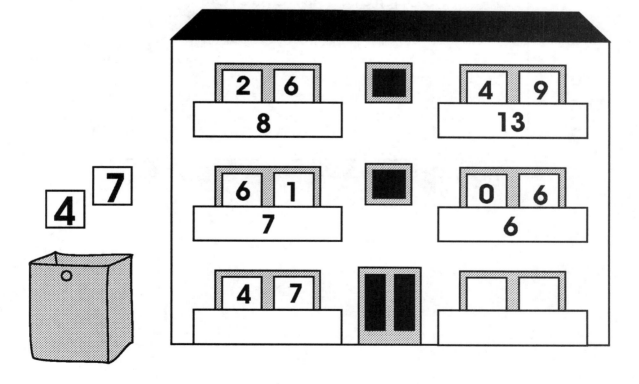

Geometry and Spatial Relationships

Robot Shapes
Alphabet Symmetry
Half and Half
Coordinate Points
Bicycle Parts
Star Stack
Congruent Characters
Right, Left

Robot Shapes

Pattern: Robot, page 292

292

Give each student a copy of the robot pattern. Challenge students to count the number of rectangles and squares. Invite students to cut the rectangles and squares apart and then reconstruct the robot. Encourage students to add other construction-paper shapes, such as triangles and circles to create a new-and-improved robot.

Alphabet Symmetry

Pattern: Alphabet, page 325

325

Give each student a copy of the letter patterns and a small mirror. Challenge students to discover which letters are symmetrical (look the same on both sides). Have students place a mirror on the line of symmetry. As students look at half of the letter on the paper and half of the letter in the mirror, the letter should look complete.

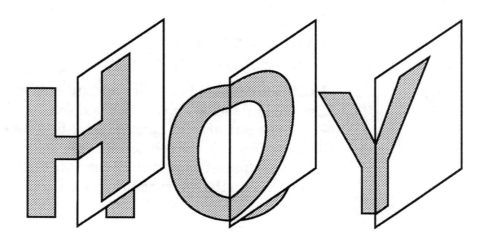

Half and Half
Patterns: Apartment, page 220; Bed, page 221; Two-Story House, page 225; Pineapple, page 257; Robot, page 292; School, page 237; Airplane, page 192; Traffic Signal, page 191; Maple Leaf, page 2; Corn, page 5; Daisy, page 16; Jack-o'-Lantern, page 33; Scarecrow, page 35; Sailor, page 40

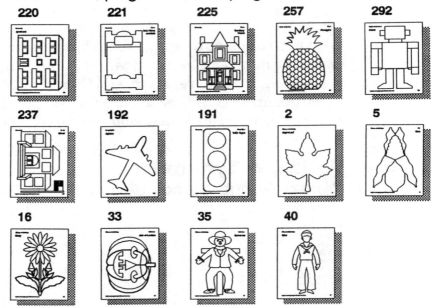

Give each student half of one of the symmetrical patterns. Invite each student to glue the half to a sheet of tagboard. Challenge the children to try drawing the missing half of the pattern. To make the symmetry drawings reusable, cover the cards with clear acetate. Have the cards available at the math center.

Coordinate Points
Patterns: Any patterns

Invite students to help color and cut out ten patterns of your choosing. Draw a horizontal and vertical axis on the chalkboard. Add grid lines. Place the patterns at random grid-line intersections. Challenge students to identify the coordinate points for the patterns you name. Or, distribute patterns and challenge students to come to the board and place them in the appropriate spots as you name the coordinate points.

Bicycle Parts

Pattern: Bicycle, page 193

193

Give each child a copy of the bicycle pattern. Write the following directions on the chalkboard or give them orally.

> Find the two largest circles and color them black.
>
> Color all the other circles red.
>
> How many circles did you find altogether?
>
> How many rectangles can you find?
>
> Color the rectangles yellow.
>
> How many spokes are on the bicycle altogether?
>
> How many triangle shapes can you find in the picture?
>
> Are there any squares on the bicycle? If so, where?

Star Stack

Pattern: Stars, page 49

49

This mind-bending exercise will encourage students to use their skills of logic and reasoning while working with concentric shapes. Trace three different-sized stars on a sheet of drawing paper. Duplicate the sheet and give a set of stars to each student. Invite students to cut out the stars. Give each student three paper plates. Ask students to place the plates in a horizontal row across their desk tops. Have students stack the stars (largest on the bottom and smallest on top) and place the stack in the paper plate on their left. Challenge students to transfer the stack to the paper plate on the right following a few simple rules. Students can only move one star at a time from plate to plate. A larger star can never be placed on top of a smaller one. After children have experienced success, challenge them to try the activity again using four stars. The same rules apply.

Congruent Characters

Patterns: Cat, page 129; Kitten, page 136; Collie, page 131; German Shepherd, page 135; Puppy, page 139; Scottie and Beagle, page 140

129 **136**  **131**  **135**  **139**  **140**

Trace each pattern onto black construction paper. Cut the silhouette characters out and mount them on construction paper. Duplicate, color, and cut out the same patterns as the silhouettes. Then laminate both the silhouettes and the matching characters (or cover with clear adhesive-backed paper) and place them at the math center. Remind students that *congruent* is the word we use to describe two figures that are exactly the same size and shape. Challenge children to match the congruent shapes.

Right, Left

Pattern: Mitten, page 14

14

Make several cardboard mitten patterns by tracing and cutting the mitten from tagboard. Invite each child to use a pattern to trace and cut four mittens from construction paper. Help children match and staple the edges of the mittens together to make a pair. Leave the wrist ends open so children can actually wear their paper mittens. Help the children write the words *left* and *right* on the appropriate mittens. Give children directions to follow as they wear their mittens.

Place your right mitten high in the air.

Place your left mitten behind your back.

Place your right mitten on top of your left mitten.

...d Money

...ng the Price
...ick Tock Twos
Making a Million
Math Path
Time Match
Pricey Presents
The Price Is Right
More or Less
Beat the Clock

Thank You!
Rita
Books for a Cause

Paying the Price
Pattern: Money, page 324

324

Give each child two copies of the money pattern page. Invite children to color the money using appropriate colors. Have children cut out the coins and glue them back-to-back so the money is double sided. Place all the money in a box at the math center. Attach price tags to magazine pictures or other patterns. Encourage children to role play being store owners and customers as they pay for items and make change.

Tick Tock Twos
Pattern: Clock, page 65

65

Give each child a copy of the clock pattern. Invite children to cut out the clock face and hands. Have children glue the clock faces to 7" tagboard circles. Help each child attach the hands with a paper fastener. Encourage children to work in pairs to practice telling time. One partner can position the clock hands and challenge the other partner to tell or write the correct time. Or, one partner can challenge the other to position the clock hands to an indicated time. Encourage partners to switch roles.

Making a Million
Pattern: Money, page 324

324

Read *If You Made a Million* by David M. Schwartz (New York: Lothrop, Lee & Shepard, 1989) to your students. Assign daily salary rates to classroom jobs, such as paper monitor, line leader, and messenger. Invite students to fill out job applications. Hire candidates to fill the positions for one-week periods. Pay students according to the salary rates agreed upon using the money patterns. Encourage students to calculate how much money they have made at the end of a designated period of time. Challenge students to consider how long it would take them to make a million dollars.

Math Path

Pattern: Money, page 324

324

Give each child a money pattern page to color and cut out. Remind students to use appropriate colors so the money is identifiable. Collect the money and place random amounts on each student's desk. Also place a numbered card on each student's desk to designate a math path. For example, the student's desk in the front of the room would be desk #1, the desk beside that would be #2, and so on down the rows. Give each student an answer sheet with as many numbered blank lines as there are numbered desks. Invite students to begin at their own desk and add up the amount of money placed there. Have students write their answers in the appropriate blanks on their answer sheets. For example, if a student begins at desk #8, he or she writes the amount of money at that desk on blank #8. When each student has had enough time to add up the money and write down an answer, give a signal for students to move to the next desk. The student in desk #8 would move to desk #9 and so on. Students again total the amount of money at the desk and write the answer in the appropriate blank. Students continue moving through the math path on the given signal until they reach the desk in which they started. Check the answers together as a class.

Time Match

Patterns: Clock, page 65; Toothpaste and Toothbrush, page 243; Beef Dinner, page 245; School, page 237; Bed, page 221; Sun, page 25

65   **243**   **245**   **237**   **221**   **25**

  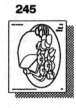 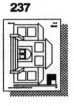 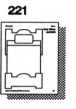 

Give each child a copy of the clock pattern. Invite each child to cut out the clock face and hands. Have children glue the clock faces to 7" tagboard circles. Help children attach the hands with paper fasteners. Invite each child to face a partner. Hold up a picture pattern as a cue and ask students to position the clock hands to an appropriate time. For example, hold up the sun and ask students what time the sun rises. After students have positioned the hands, invite them to compare with their partners. If the two partners have the same time, the team earns a point. Continue holding up pictures and asking partners to position the clock hands as they try to make time matches.

Pricey Presents

Pattern: Present, page 56

56

Give each student a present pattern. Invite children to color and cut out the presents and attach price tags. Divide the class into small groups of five or six. Challenge students to put their gifts in order according to price from the least expensive to the most expensive. Provide several other tasks for each group to accomplish using the pricey presents, such as calculate the difference in price between the least and most expensive gifts, find the total of all the presents combined, and guess what might be inside each gift based on its price tag.

The Price Is Right

Patterns: Banana, page 254; Rake, page 284; Bicycle, page 193;
Crayons, page 234; Car, page 195

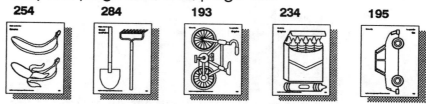

Write a price on a 3" x 5" card to match each picture pattern. Laminate
or cover the price cards and picture patterns with clear adhesive-
backed paper and place them at the math center. Challenge students
to match sensible prices to the correct pictures. Write the correct prices
on the back of the pictures to add a self-checking feature. Select other
patterns and prices as well to change the center.

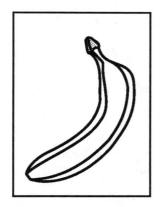

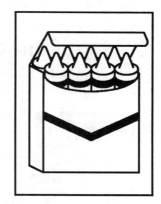

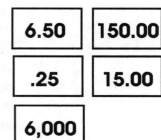

More or Less

Pattern: Money, page 324

324

Color several money pattern pages and make overhead transparencies from them. Cut the money out. Write an amount of money on the chalkboard, such as $1.34. Place some transparency coins and dollar bills on an overhead projector so everyone can see them. Invite students to put their thumbs up if the amount on the overhead is more than the amount written on the chalkboard and their thumbs down if the amount is less. Change the amount of money on the overhead several times and ask for a "thumbs up" or "thumbs down" response. Change the amount of money written on the chalkboard from time to time as well.

Beat the Clock

Pattern: Numbers, page 325

325

Use the number patterns to make small number cards from 1 to 12. Laminate the cards or cover them with clear adhesive-backed paper. Place the number cards in the math center with a large cardboard circle. In pairs, invite students to use the materials to play "Beat the Clock." One partner estimates how long it will take him or her to arrange the number cards around the cardboard circle to represent a clock face. The other partner times the task. Students can compare the estimates with the actual amount of time it takes to complete the task correctly.

Science

Animals

Wild Animal Collage
Koala Capers
Porcupine Prickles
Animal Twister
Pet Premiere
Animal Rubs
Endangered Species
A Frog's Life
The Same Yet Different
Dinosaur World Shadow Box
Are You My Mother?

Wild Animal Collage

Patterns: Brown Bear, page 95; Alligator, page 91; Polar Bear, page 118; Penguin, page 145; Giraffe, page 105; Rhinoceros, page 122; Zebra, page 128; Gorilla, page 106; Buffalo, page 96; Whale, page 153; Koala, page 109; African Elephant, page 101; Hippopotamus, page 107; Tiger, page 125; Giant Panda, page 116; Kangaroo, page 108; Seal, page 147; Llama, page 112

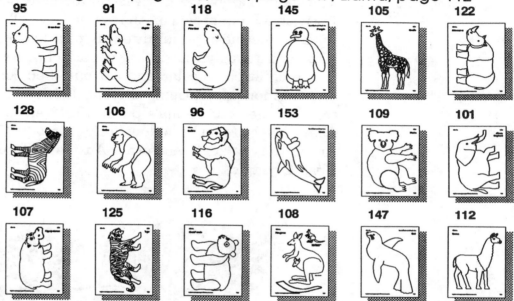

Show children the torn construction-paper illustrations of the wild animals in *My First Wild Animals* by Bettina Patterson (Harper Collins, 1991). Give each child a wild animal pattern and a variety of colors of construction paper. Invite children to tear construction paper shapes in appropriate colors and sizes to glue to the wild animal patterns. Encourage children to use resource books to find out fascinating facts about their animals to share with the class.

Koala Capers
Pattern: Koala, page 109

109

The koala is known as the Australian teddy bear. It has thick ash-grey fur with a bit of brown on the upper parts. The koala lives most of its life in a tree and eats mainly eucalyptus leaves. Invite children to place a koala in a eucalyptus tree. Give each child a copy of the koala pattern. Invite children to color and cut out their koalas and glue them on construction paper. Using crayons, help each child draw a eucalyptus tree between the Koala's paws. Children might also enjoy hearing *Koala Lou* by Mem Fox (New York: Harcourt Brace Jovanovich, 1988). In the story, a koala and other Australian animals participate in the Bush Olympics.

Porcupine Prickles

Pattern: Porcupine, page 119

119

The porcupine has strong stiff quills on its back, sides, and tail. Porcupines defend themselves by striking with their quilled tails. Give each child a copy of the porcupine pattern. Invite children to color and cut out the porcupines. Help children glue toothpicks on the porcupine's back and tail to remind them of the porcupine's defense system.

Animal Twister

Patterns: Anteater, page 92; Armadillo, page 93; Buffalo, page 96; Giraffe, page 105; Llama, page 112; Moose, page 114; Ostrich, page 115; Quail, page 120; Rhinoceros, page 122

Use a permanent marker to divide a plastic drop cloth into nine squares. Glue an 8 1/2" x 11" clear plastic sheet protector to each square. Reproduce the animal patterns, color them, and cut them out. Mount each animal on an 8 1/2" x 11" sheet of construction paper. Slip a picture inside each sheet protector mounted on the drop cloth. Give students directions (or make task cards) for playing "Animal Twister." Encourage the children to play the game in stocking feet or without socks. For example, direct a student to place his or her right foot on the moose, left elbow on the llama, and right knee on the giraffe. Remind students to retain each previous position while following the new direction. For variety, slip the animal cards out of the pockets and replace them with food cards, transportation cards, or flower cards.

Pet Premiere

Patterns: Cat, page 129; Cockatoo, page 130; Collie, page 131; Fish, page 132; Gerbil, page 134; German Shepherd, page 135; Mouse, page 137; Poodle, page 138; Scottie and Beagle, page 140;

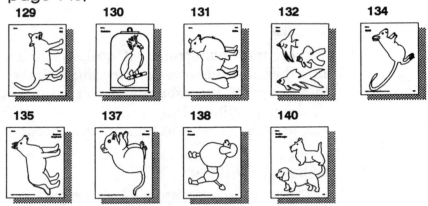

Reproduce the pet patterns, color them, and cut them out. Mount each pet on an 8 1/2" x 11" sheet of construction paper. Use the same color for each pattern. Invite a child to come to the front of the room and choose a pet pattern from the deck. Encourage the child to give a clue about the animal's identity. The clues might include what the animal eats, where it sleeps, what it has been trained to do, or a description of a physical characteristic. Invite other classmates to guess which animal is being described. If no one guesses correctly, encourage the child to give another clue. Encourage students to begin with hard clues before giving ones that make the animal's identity more obvious.

Animal Rubs

Patterns: Alligator, page 91; Armadillo, page 93; Brown Bear, page 95; Crocodile, page 99; African Elephant, page 101; Hippopotamus, page 107; Lizard, page 111; Bald Eagle, page 171; Woodpecker, page 172

91   **93**   **95**   **99**   **101**

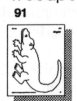    

107 **111** **171** **172**

Many animals and birds have uniquely textured fur, scales, or feathers. Invite each child to choose an animal pattern and find a textured surface that might make an interesting design. Help children place their animal patterns over the textured surfaces and then rub over the papers with the sides of crayons.

Endangered Species

Patterns: Blue Whale, page 141; Crocodile, page 99; Rhinoceros, page 122; California Condor, page 97

141 **99** **122** **97**

Endangered species are living things that are threatened with extinction. Thousands of animals are on the endangered list and the number increases each year. Endangered species include blue whales, some kinds of crocodiles, rhinoceroses, and the California condor. Help your students become aware of the danger these animals face by discussing some of the reasons for endangerment, such as destruction of habitat or overhunting. Encourage students to think of ways we could better protect these animals. Give each student a copy of one of the endangered animal patterns. Invite students to color and cut out their animals and use them to create displays, posters, or brochures with some possible solutions to the problem.

A Frog's Life

Pattern: Frog Life Cycle, page 103

103

When the female frog first lays her eggs, the eggs sink to the bottom of the pond. Then they float back to the surface among the weeds or scum at the water's edge. The tadpole that comes from the egg does not look anything like a frog. But soon the tadpole grows a pair of hind legs and then a pair of front legs. The tadpole's gills gradually close and the frog develops lungs. Encourage students to color and cut out the life cycle patterns and glue them in order on construction paper. Invite students to write or dictate sentences that describe each stage. Children might also enjoy hearing the story of *The Mysterious Tadpole* by Steven Kellogg (New York: Dial, 1977). In this imaginative tale, Louis begins with a tadpole in a jar and ends up with a green creature with pink polka dots.

The Same Yet Different

Patterns: Fish, page 132; Blue Whale, page 141; Saltwater Fish, page 152; Whale, page 153; Shark, page 151; Collie, page 131; German Shepherd, page 135; Poodle, page 138; Puppy, page 139, Scottie and Beagle, page 140; Bald Eagle, page 171; Woodpecker, page 172; Blue Jay, page 173; Hummingbird, page 174; Sea Gull, page 156; Pelican, page 154; Penguin, page 145; Ostrich, page 115

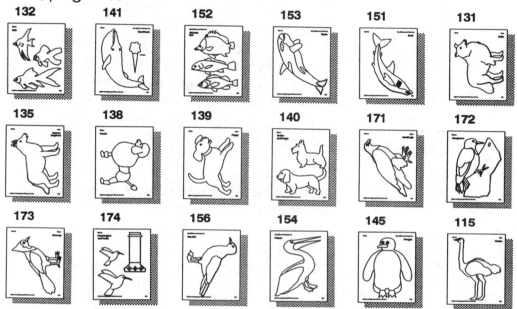

Invite children to help color and cut out the animal patterns. Mount each dog pattern on a piece of green construction paper. Mount the sea creatures on blue construction paper and mount the birds on red construction paper. Invite children to work in groups at the science center. Encourage each child in turn to choose two cards that are mounted on the same color of construction paper. Invite each child to point out some similarities and differences between the two pictures.

Dinosaur World Shadow Box

Patterns: Brontosaurus, page 185; Stegosaurus, page 186; Triceratops, page 187; Tyrannosaurus, page 188

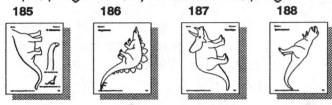

Make a large dinosaur exhibit by enlarging the patterns and cutting them out of posterboard. Divide the class into four groups and give each group a large dinosaur to paint. Help children attach pieces of cardboard to the backs of the patterns so the dinosaurs will stand. Invite students to glue crushed newspaper inside the bottom of a large appliance box tipped on its side. Help students paint the newspaper mounds green or brown to represent hills and rocks.

Are You My Mother?

Patterns: Rabbit and Bunny, page 160; Cow and Calf, page 161; Mare and Foal, page 163; Ewe and Lamb, page 164; Sow and Piglet, page 165; Hen and Chicks, page 166; Duck and Ducklings, page 168; Mother and Baby Birds, page 176

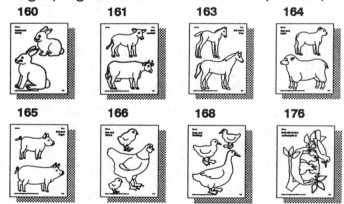

Reproduce each pattern. Invite children to help color and cut out the patterns. Mount the pictures on construction-paper squares. Turn all the pictures over on a table. Encourage children to take turns turning over two pictures at a time to find matching adult and baby animals. When children find matching pairs, encourage them to name the animals.

Birds and Insects
Beautiful Butterflies
Honeybee Homes
Hardworking Ants
Ladybug on a String
Home Sweet Nest
Ostrich Eggs

Beautiful Butterflies

Pattern: Butterfly, page 180

180

Give each child a butterfly pattern. Invite children to cut out the butterflies and sponge paint both sides in a variety of bright colors. After the paint dries, help each child glue a spring-type clothespin over the butterfly body section between the wings. Children can clip the butterflies to their clothing, on a notebook, or on a curtain or window shade. Children might also enjoy hearing the story *I Wish I Were a Butterfly* by James Howe (New York: Harcourt Brace Jovanovich, 1987).

Honeybee Homes

Pattern: Hive and Honeybee, page 179

179

Honeybees live in beehives which contain individual honeycombs with cells of beeswax. The honeybee is considered one of our most useful insects. In the United States alone about 5 million colonies annually produce $50 million worth of honey and beeswax. Invite children to make honeycombs by stacking and gluing empty toilet tissue rolls together in a pyramid shape. Children can color, cut out, and glue bees to the sticky home.

Hardworking Ants

Pattern: Ant, page 182

182

Ants, like other insects, have three body parts and six legs. Although we generally think of ants as pests they are truly remarkable scavengers and hard workers. Give each student an ant to color and cut out. Display the ants on a bulletin board entitled "Hard Work Makes the Grade." Staple the ants going up a hill and display some examples of your students' excellent work at the top. Children might enjoy the story *Two Bad Ants* by Chris Van Allsburg (Boston: Houghton Mifflin, 1988). In the story, two ants experience danger when they leave the safety of their colony. They soon become convinced that home is where they belong.

Ladybug on a String

Pattern: Ladybug, page 178

178

The ladybug goes through a metamorphosis much like a butterfly does. When it emerges from its pupa, the ladybug does not yet have its well-recognized spots. It is soft and orange. When the ladybug's wings harden and dry the spots begin to appear. Give each child a ladybug pattern to color and cut out. Have children cut off the six ladybug legs and replace them with accordion pleated construction-paper strips. Help each child tape a piece of yarn or thread to the ladybug's back. Hang the ladybugs from your classroom ceiling.

Home Sweet Nest

Patterns: Bald Eagle, page 171; Hummingbird, page 174; Woodpecker, page 172

171   **174**  **172**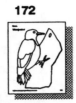

Display a real bird's nest, if possible. Discuss different types of nests built by different birds. A bald eagle's nest can become as large as eight feet across because each year the eagle couple adds to and repairs the same nest. A hummingbird's nest is no bigger than a thimble. A woodpecker makes a nest by chipping out a tunnel in a tree trunk with its beak. Give each student a copy of the bird patterns. Invite students to color and cut out the birds. Encourage students to make nests that are appropriate for each bird. For example, a hole cut in the side of an empty paper towel tube could simulate a woodpecker's tree trunk home. Encourage creativity and provide students opportunities to work in groups and brainstorm ideas.

Ostrich Eggs

Pattern: Ostrich, page 115; Eggs (Easter Eggs), page 83

115   **83**

Ostriches, the largest birds in the world, produce the world's biggest eggs. Ostrich eggs are about the size of a football. The shell is so strong that an adult man could stand on it without cracking it. Invite each child to cut an egg from construction paper about the size of a football. Invite children to color and cut out an ostrich pattern and glue it beside the large egg. Encourage students to find out about other bird egg sizes.

Environment

Spin a Habitat
Rainforest
Pond Life
Desert Shadow Box
The Wonderful Woods
Above the Clouds
Rainbow Ribbons

Spin a Habitat

Patterns: Deer, page 100; Raccoon, page 121; Fox, page 104; Woodpecker, page 172; Wolf, page 127; Giraffe, page 105; Gorilla, page 106; Crocodile, page 99; Rhinoceros, page 122; Zebra, page 128; Lizard, page 111; Tortoise, page 126; Quail, page 120; Dolphin, page 142; Lobster, page 143; Octopus, page 144; Seal, page 147; Shark, page 151

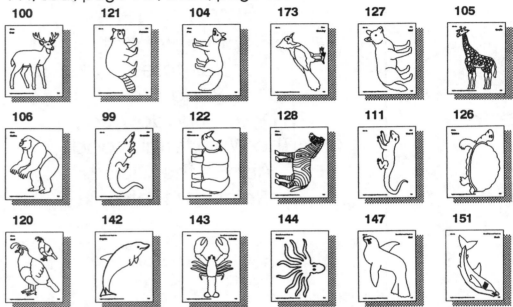

A habitat is where an animal or plant lives. It is only a good home when it is the right temperature and supplies food, water, and shelter. Cut out a cardboard spinner. Divide it into four parts (forest, desert, jungle, ocean). Use a two-pronged metal fastener to attach a cardboard arrow. Finally, make a giant gameboard on the floor of your classroom or play area. Place animal patterns along a trail. Pick animals from each habitat and place them at random along the path. Invite players to take turns spinning the cardboard spinner. Each player moves to the next animal that lives in the habitat selected by the spinner. The winner is the first person to reach the end of the trail. Reduce the animals to make a regular tabletop-size gameboard.

Rainforest

Patterns: Honeybee, page 179; Monkey, page 113; Cockatoo, page 130; Frog, page 102; Porcupine, page 119; Anteater, page 92; Butterfly, page 180

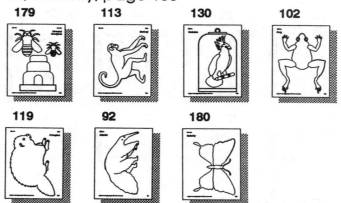

Read *The Great Kapok Tree* by Lynne Cherry (New York: Harcourt Brace Jovanovich, 1990) to your students. Through the text and illustrations, students will have a better understanding of this incredible environment, the community of animals that live there, and the importance of preserving it. Make a rainforest mural that depicts the layers of life, including the canopy and the understory. Invite students to paint a lush background using green fingerpaint. While the paint dries, invite children to color and cut out the bird and animal patterns. Help children glue the creatures among the leaves, branches, and shrubs of the tropical rainforest.

Pond Life

Patterns: Water Lily on Pad, page 18; Frogs, page 102-103; Tortoise, page 126; Duck and Ducklings, page 168; Raccoon, page 121; Beaver, 94

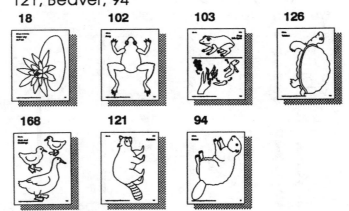

Cover the background of a bulletin board with white butcher paper. Cut a large piece of blue butcher paper to represent a pond. Cut a large sun from yellow and orange construction paper and place it in one corner of the bulletin board. Using brown paint, add a shore line around the pond. Spears of slender-stalked cattails often fringe a pond. Help children make slender green stalks from construction paper and add to them a velvety brown head that looks like a hotdog. Display the cattails along the pond's edge. Invite children to add grass, rocks, and twigs to the pond's shore. Give each student an animal pattern. Invite children to color and cut out their pond dwellers and add them to the display.

Desert Shadow Box

Patterns: Cactus, page 24; Rabbit, page 160; Owl, page 38; Woodpecker, page 172

Give each group of students a cardboard box to create a desert scene. Have children tip the box on its side with the open end facing forward.

Invite children to color and cut out several cacti. Help children fold a tab at the base of each cactus and glue the tab to the bottom of the shadow box. Reduce the animal patterns. Then invite the children to color and cut out the patterns. Add the animals to the desert scene. Encourage children to add other creative touches, such as a sandy floor made of sandpaper or a snake molded from clay.

The Wonderful Woods

Patterns: Squirrel, page 124; Acorn and Oakleaf, page 1; Raccoon, page 121; Owl, page 38; Woodpecker, page 172; Nest with Mother and Baby Birds, page 176; Butterfly, page 180; Deer, page 100; Porcupine, page 119; Bald Eagle, page 171; Blue Jay, page 173; Fox, page 104; Brown Bear, page 95

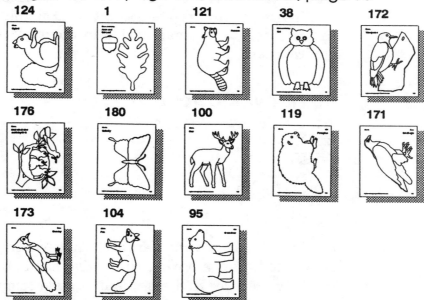

Use the patterns to create a bulletin board entitled, "The Wonderful Woods." Cover the background with white butcher paper. Draw several large tree trunks that extend off the top of the bulletin board to represent the giant trees in the forest. Invite children to color and cut out leaves to add to the forest floor. Invite children to color and cut out other patterns to add to the mural. Enlarge patterns as necessary to create proper perspective.

Above the Clouds

Patterns: Astronaut, page 210; Space Shuttle, page 205; Airplane, page 192; Helicopter, page 197; Stars, page 49

210 **205** **192**  **197** 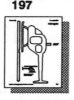 **49**

Cover a bulletin board with blue or black butcher paper. Glue a blanket of white clouds made from cotton along the bottom of the paper. Cut a moon from white construction paper and display it in one corner of the bulletin board. Show the children how to use glitter to make sparkly stars or cut aluminum foil into star shapes. Enlarge the other patterns and invite the children to decorate and cut out the figures. Encourage the children to be imaginative in creating their upper atmosphere environment.

Rainbow Ribbons

Pattern: Rainbow, page 22

22

A rainbow is a beautiful part of the natural environment and can often be spotted after a spring rain. Give each student two copies of the rainbow pattern. Invite students to use tempera paint to color each arch, beginning with the outer arch—red, orange, yellow, green, blue, indigo, violet. Children can shake glitter onto the wet paint to add a sparkly touch. After the paint has dried, have children cut out both rainbows and glue them back-to-back with a popsicle stick in between the patterns. Invite children to cut 1/2"-wide strips of construction paper the same colors as the rainbow arches. Help children attach the ribbon strips to the ends of the rainbows, between the two pattern pieces.

Nutrition

Fun Fruits
Invent a Cereal
Apples and Pumpkins
Matching Wholes and Halves
Hoagies and Heros
Vegetable Garden
Food Groups
Food Place Mats
Fruit and Vegetable Sort

Fun Fruits

Patterns: Orange and Grapefruit, page 248; Lemon and Apple, page 249; Peach, page 250; Apricot and Pear, page 251; Grapes, page 253; Banana, page 254; Strawberry (Berries), page 255; Pineapple, page 257; Watermelon, page 258; Cantaloupe, page 259

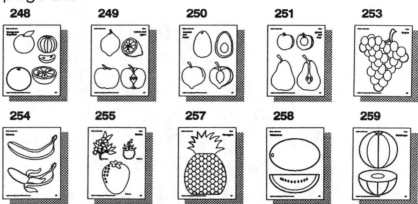

Fruits are not only delicious to eat, but they are also important for health. Invite children to help make this fun fruit display as a reminder that fruit should be an important part of everyone's diets. Give each child a fruit pattern to color or trace and cut from construction paper. Invite children to draw faces on their fruits. Children can cut narrow strips from construction paper to make arms and legs. Help children accordion pleat the strips and staple or glue in place. Display the fun fruits on a bulletin board.

Invent a Cereal

Pattern: Box and Bowl of Cereal, page 272

Grains are an important component of a balanced diet. Cereals are often made from corn, wheat, or rice. However, many cereals have an excessive amount of sugar added to them. Invite children to look closely at the labels of their favorite cereals. The closer sugar is to the top of the ingredients list, the more sugar the cereal has. Challenge students to find three cereals with sugar as one of the top three ingredients and three cereals with sugar near the end of the ingredients list. Invite children to invent new brands of nutritious cereals and design boxes with appropriate words and pictures. Give each child a copy of the cereal box and bowl pattern. Encourage children to use construction paper to make cereal shapes to fill the cereal bowls. Invite children to promote their cereals by explaining to the class their nutritional value and benefits.

Apples and Pumpkins

Patterns: Apple, page 249; Pumpkin, page 6

249   **6**

Read *Apples and Pumpkins* by Anne Rockwell (New York: Macmillan, 1989) to your students. In the story, a family picks shiny red apples and a beautiful orange pumpkin from the field. Invite children to think of ways they enjoy eating apples (applesauce, apple muffins, apple pie) and pumpkins (pumpkin pie, pumpkin cookies, pumpkin bread). Encourage children to bring in recipes from home that use apples or pumpkin as the main ingredient. Help each student make an apple or pumpkin shape booklet by cutting two identical food patterns from construction paper to make a front and back cover. Invite children to cut lined paper in the same shape to place between the covers. Write some of the recipes students bring from home on chart paper or the chalkboard. Encourage students to copy the recipes into their shape booklets. Children can take the booklets home and share the recipes with their families.

Matching Wholes and Halves

Patterns: Orange and Grapefruit, page 248; Lemon and Apple, page 249; Avocado and Peach, page 250; Apricot and Pear, page 251; Watermelon, page 258; Cantaloupe, page 259

248  **249**  **250** 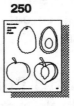 **251** 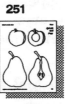 **258**  **259**

If possible, have the actual fruits in the pattern list available for students to examine. Invite students to predict what the fruits will look like when cut open. Ask students to predict how many seeds they will have and what size the seeds will be. Give each pair of students the fruit patterns to color and cut out. Challenge students to work in pairs to match the wholes with the halves. Students may enjoy timing how long it takes each student to make the matches and then try to beat the individual records.

Hoagies and Heros

Pattern: Bread, page 273

273

Brainstorm a list of words that are synonymous with a large sandwich (hoagie, hero, submarine, grinder, poor boy, torpedo). Encourage students to explain how they make their favorite sandwiches. Give each student a copy of the bread slice pattern. Invite students to trace and cut two bread slices from brown or white construction paper. Encourage students to cut shapes from appropriately colored construction paper to make foods to put between their two slices of bread to create delicious and nutritious sandwiches. Your students might also enjoy hearing the story of the *Giant Jam Sandwich* by John Vernon Lord (Boston: Houghton Mifflin, 1972). The residents of a small town construct a giant sandwich filled with delicious strawberry jam to capture unwanted insects.

Vegetable Garden

Patterns: Corn, page 5; Pumpkin, page 6; Squash, page 7; Green Beans and Peas, page 256; Tomato and Carrot, page 261; Cauliflower, page 262; Lettuce, page 263; Zucchini and Broccoli, page 264; Onions, page 265; Beet and Cucumber, page 266; Celery, Radish, and Bell Pepper, page 267; Yam and Potato, page 268

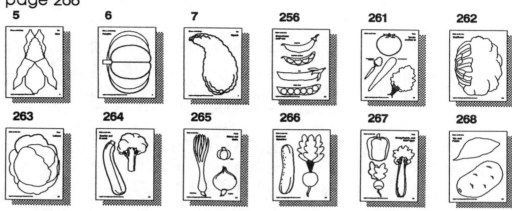

Cover the bottom half of a bulletin board with brown butcher paper. Give each child one or two vegetable patterns to color and cut out. Help children staple the vegetables onto the bulletin-board garden. Help children place the vegetables above or below the ground level to show where they grow. Encourage children to add roots, vines, leaves, fences, and other details to the bulletin-board display using crayons, markers, or paint. Discuss the nutritional value of vegetables. The bulletin board could be entitled, "A Garden to Grow On."

Food Groups

Patterns: Food patterns, pages 245-273

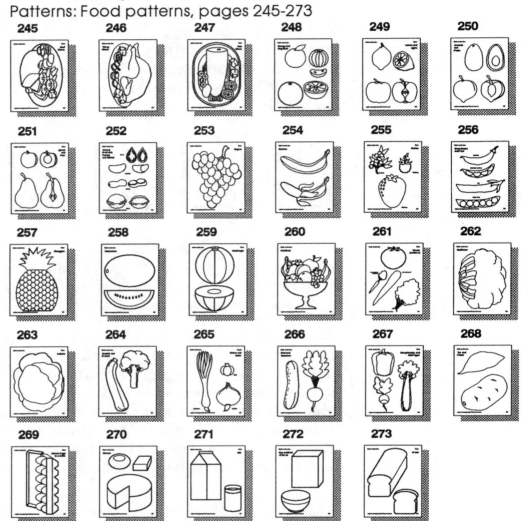

Divide a long sheet of butcher paper into five sections. Label each section with one of the five food groups based on the USDA Food Guide Pyramid —milk, yogurt, and cheese; meat, poultry, fish, beans, eggs, and nuts; vegetables; fruits; bread, cereal, rice, and pasta. Give each student a food pattern to color and cut out. Invite students to place the foods in the appropriate groups.

Food Place Mats

Patterns: Food patterns, pages 245-273

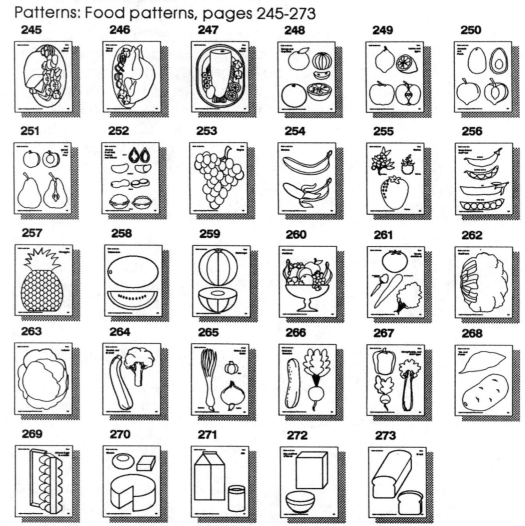

Invite children to choose several of their favorite foods from the patterns. Encourage children to color the patterns with crayons and cut them out. Help children place the food pictures between two sheets of wax paper. Press carefully with a warm iron. Trim the edges with pinking shears. Invite children to take their place mats home.

Fruit and Vegetable Sort

Patterns: Orange and Grapefruit, page 248; Lemon and Apple, page 249; Peach, page 250; Apricot and Pear, page 251; Grapes, page 253; Banana, page 254; Strawberry, page 255; Pineapple, page 257; Watermelon, page 258; Cantaloupe, page 259; Corn, page 5; Pumpkin, page 6; Squash, page 7; Green Beans and Peas, page 256; Tomato and Carrot, page 261; Cauliflower, page 262; Lettuce, page 263; Zucchini and Broccoli, page 264; Onions, page 265; Beet and Cucumber, page 266; Celery, Radish, and Bell Pepper, page 267; Yam and Potato, page 268

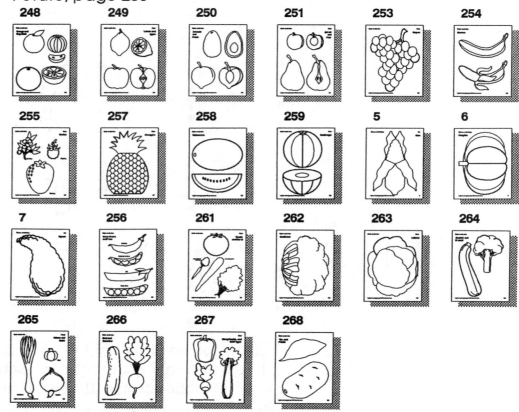

Give each child a fruit or vegetable pattern. Invite children to trace and cut the shapes from construction paper. Laminate the shapes or cover them with clear adhesive-backed paper. Place the fruits and vegetables in the science learning center. Encourage students to sort the foods in several ways. Students can sort the foods into fruit or vegetable groups. Students can group the foods to show which ones they have tasted and which ones they have not. Or, students could group the foods by color or size.

Ocean Life

Octopus Alive!
Lobster on the Loose
Penguins on Parade
Image Upgrade
Sea Life Bingo
Sea Life Mural
Indoor Sea Adventure
Deep-Sea Scenes

Octopus Alive!

Pattern: Octopus, page 144

144

An octopus has eight arms and a short, rounded body. Many octopuses live on the ocean floor where they hide among rocks and grab passing creatures with their long, suckered arms. Octopuses propel themselves through the water by squirting water from their bodies. Give each child two copies of the octopus pattern. Encourage children to color the octopus patterns and cut them out. Invite children to glue the arms of the two patterns together leaving the body and head open. Help children stuff the body and head with tissue paper and then staple the edges together. Children can curl the octopus arms by wrapping them around a pencil. Display the octopuses on a bulletin board covered with blue butcher paper. Encourage children to add other details to the deep-sea display using crayons, paint, or construction paper. Students might enjoy reading *I Was All Thumbs* by Bernard Waber (Boston: Houghton Mifflin, 1975). In the story, a loveable yet clumsy octopus finds everyday life a bit difficult in the deep ocean waters.

Lobster on the Loose

Pattern: Lobster, page 143

143

Lobsters are marine animals that live in all oceans of the world. They belong to a group of animals called *crustaceans*. They are covered with a hard shell and breathe through gills. Lobsters also belong to a group called *decapods* because they have ten legs. Lobsters have two front legs with large claws. Trace the lobster body parts onto another sheet of paper so they are in random order. Reproduce the page and give each child a set of lobster parts. Invite children to cut out the body parts and glue them on sheets of paper to make lobsters.

Penguins on Parade

Pattern: Penguin, page 145

145

Most people think of penguins as birds of ice and snow. Although some live in the Antarctica, many live in warmer climates closer to the equator. But, all penguins live in the Southern Hemisphere. Penguins range in size from 16 inches to 3 1/2 feet tall. These birds do not fly and spend most of their lives in the water. Their black and white tuxedo-style coloring helps them hide in the sea. Their black backs blend into the darkness of the water. From below, their white undersides are hard to see against the sky. Help each child correctly color and cut out a penguin pattern. Help children make small stick banners for their penguins to hold that convey some interesting facts about penguins. For example, a poster might show a globe with a big X in the Southern Hemisphere and "X marks the spot" written below it. Display the banner-toting penguins in a parade line on a bulletin board.

Image Upgrade

Pattern: Shark, page 151

151

Sharks have a bad reputation, but of the 200 varieties only 25 are in fact dangerous to people. Invite children to research sharks to learn why it is an important member of the ocean family. Have students use this information to improve the shark's image by designing promotional buttons and posters that present the shark in a positive light.

Sea Life Bingo

Patterns: Octopus, page 144; Penguin, page 145; Sea Horse, page 146; Shark, page 151; Seal, page 147; Pelican, page 154; Dolphin, page 142; Lobster, page 143; Whale, page 153; Sea Gull, page 156; Sea Turtle, page 150

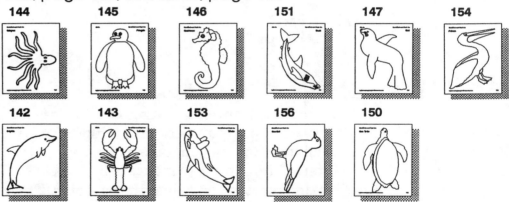

Give each student a bingo card with nine squares. Write the name of each sea creature pattern on the chalkboard. Invite students to copy one name in each of their nine squares. Encourage students to write the names in random order so that each student's card is different. Give each student a supply of bingo markers—beans, paper clips, paper squares. Hold up one of the sea creature patterns for students to identify. If the student has that word on his or her card, the square is covered with a marker. The first player to correctly identify and cover a row of sea creatures on his or her card shouts, "Bingo."

Sea Life Mural

Patterns: Sea Animals, pages 141-153

Invite students to use blue fingerpaint to make interesting ocean designs on a large sheet of butcher paper. While the mural is drying, invite each student to color and cut out one sea creature. Encourage children to glue the sea creatures on the mural. Tape a card that tells some interesting fact next to each animal.

Dolphins are considered the jumping champions of the sea.

When frightened, the octopus shoots out a cloud of "ink" to hide itself.

Indoor Sea Adventure

Patterns: Blue Whale, page 141; Dolphin, page 142; Lobster, page 143; Octopus, page 144; Sea Horse, page 146; Seal, page 147; Sea Lion, page 148; Shark, page 151; Saltwater Fish, page 152; Whale, page 153

Set up a card table and hang several sea life cutouts taped to the underside of a tabletop. Cut large blue waves from construction paper and attach to three sides of the table. Cover the entire table with a sheet to create an underwater effect. Invite children to wear a pair of goggles or a swim mask and go scuba diving with a flashlight underneath the covered table.

Deep-Sea Scenes

Patterns: Sea Animals, pages 141-153

The ocean can range in depth from 6,000 feet to over 20,000 feet. Some of the most exciting mysteries and beautiful creatures live in this deep-sea environment. Encourage each child to create a deep-sea scene that displays some of these beautiful creatures. Have each child place the ink side of a used ditto facedown on a blank sheet of drawing paper. Invite each student to select a sea creature pattern and lay it on top of the ink sheet. Have students trace the patterns with pencils thereby transferring the patterns to the blank drawing sheet underneath. After tracing, remove the patterns and ink sheets. Invite children to color areas of their inked tracings by pressing heavily with crayons. Instruct children to use white crayon on any section they wish to remain uncolored. Help children dip their pictures in a shallow tray of water. The inked outline will run and spread creating a nice underwater effect. Remove the pictures from the water and allow them to dry thoroughly.

Weather and Seasons

Season Circle
Clothing Connection
Spring Fling Mobile
Summer Fun
Winter Wonderland
Fall Foliage
Wind Power
Spring in Bloom

Season Circle

Patterns: Spring Tree, page 23; Summer Tree, page 323; Fall Tree, page 322; Winter Tree, page 11

23   **323**   **322** 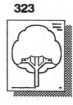 **11**

Cut a large circle from tagboard and divide it into quarters. Glue a tree in each quarter and label the season. Invite children to glue pictures cut from magazines that depict scenery in each of the four seasons.

Clothing Connection

Patterns: Snowflakes, page 12; Sun, page 25

12 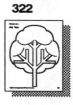 **25**

Color and cut out the snowflake and sun patterns. Glue the snowflake to the center of one posterboard and the sun to another. Discuss how clothing styles and fabrics change from season to season. Brainstorm a list of clothing appropriate for warm, sunny weather and a list of clothing appropriate for cold, snowy weather. Help children make a connection between climate and the clothing they choose to wear. Invite children to cut clothing pictures from magazines. Help children glue the pictures to the appropriate posterboards.

Spring Fling Mobile

Patterns: Daisy, page 16; Tulip, page 17; Blue Jay, page 173;
Honeybee, page 179; Butterfly, page 180

16   **17**   **173**   **179**   **180**

    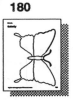

Spring is usually marked by warmer weather and the appearance of
blooming flowers, buzzing bees, and chirping birds. Give each student
a copy of each spring pattern. Invite students to color both sides of the
patterns and cut them out. Help students punch holes in the tops of the
patterns and string yarn or thread through the holes. Punch several
holes in a plastic coffee can lid for each student. Help students tie the
patterns at varying lengths from the lids to create spring-fling mobiles.

Summer Fun

Patterns: Sun, page 25; Beach Ball and Bucket, page 26; Baseball, page 294; Baseball Bat, page 295; Bicycle, page 193

25   **26**   **294**   **295**   **193**

In most areas of the country, the warm summer days and evenings are
perfect for outdoor fun. Encourage students to share their favorite
summertime outdoor activities. Give each student a copy of the sun
and a variety of outdoor activity patterns. Encourage students to color
and cut out the patterns. Invite students to glue the patterns to 12" x
18" sheets of construction paper to make summer fun collages. Encourage students to add other favorite activities to the collages by drawing
or cutting pictures from magazines.

Winter Wonderland

Pattern: Snow Person, page 9

Ask students to brainstorm a list of winter activities they enjoy. Write the ideas on the chalkboard. Give each child a 12" x 18" sheet of black and white construction paper and a snow person pattern. Invite children to tear the white construction paper on a diagonal to make a sloping hill. Help students glue the sloping hill to the black sheet of paper. Invite students to color and cut out the snow person and glue it to the hill as well. Mix a solution of half Epsom salt and half water. Invite students to dip cotton swabs in the mixture and then dab them on the black sky in their winter pictures. As the water dries, the salt crystals will create sparkly snowflakes. Encourage children to use markers or crayons to draw themselves doing a favorite winter activity on their snow-covered hill.

Fall Foliage

Patterns: Acorn and Oak Leaf, page 1; Maple Leaf, page 2;
Sycamore Leaf, page 3; Rake, page 284

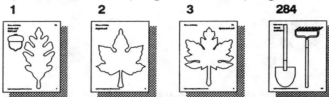

Give each student copies of the rake and several leaf patterns to cut
out. Invite students to use old toothbrushes to spatter autumn-colored
paint on the leaves—brown, orange, yellow, red. Have the children dip
the old toothbrushes into tempera paint. Show the children how to run
their fingers over the bristles to spatter the paint onto the leaf
patterns. Encourage students to mix colors and cover both sides of the
leaves. Children can color the rakes, too. Help students hang the leaves
and rakes from the ceiling, staple to a bulletin board, or decorate the
walls and doors.

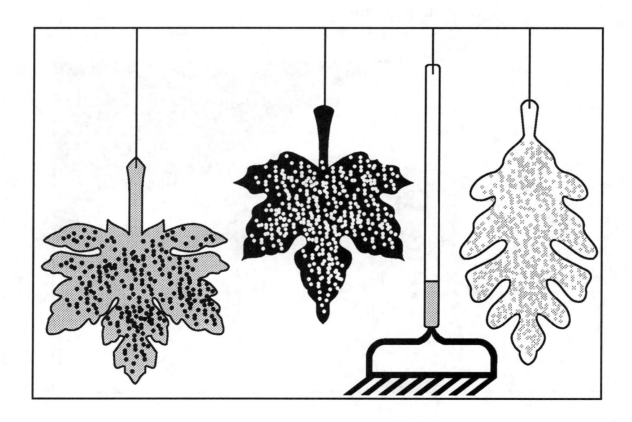

Wind Power

Patterns: Kite, page 20; Wind, page 320

20   **320**

Read *Gilberto and the Wind* by Marie Hall Ets (New York: Viking Press, 1963) to your students. In the story, Gilberto shares experiences with his unpredictable friend—Wind. He notices how the wind can blow wash on the line, invert an umbrella, power a kite, and knock ripe apples from a tree. Give students a copy of the kite and wind patterns. Invite children to color and cut out the patterns. Help children glue the wind patterns at the top of 12" x 18" sheets of construction paper in the vertical position. Encourage students to glue the kites to the poster and then draw other objects that are powered or moved by the wind, such as sailboats, hot-air balloons, wind surfers, grass, trees, or flags.

Spring in Bloom

Patterns: Sunflower, page 8; Daisy, page 16; Tulip, page 17; Rose, page 19; Honeybee, page 179; Butterfly, page 180; Snail, page 184

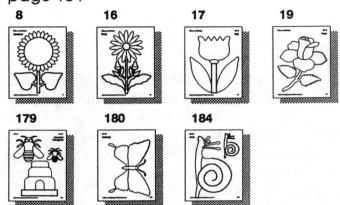

Create a large spring mural in your classroom by covering a bulletin board with blue butcher paper. Invite children to help you make grass to cover the bottom of the bulletin board using green construction-paper strips. Have children fringe the strips. Overlap the strips on the bulletin board with the fringed ends facing up towards the sky. Give each child several patterns to color and cut out. Encourage children to staple the brightly colored flowers in the grass on the bulletin board. Invite children to attach the butterfly bodies to the sky, bending the wings forward. Children can staple the snails in and among the flowers. Accordion pleat small strips of paper and glue one end to a flower and one end to a bee. Encourage children to name the flowers depicted in the mural as well as notice and identify the flowers blooming in your area.

Social Studies

People

Community Workers
Carpenter's Tool Belt
Tools of the Trade
Career Displays
World of Work
Sports Stars
People of the Past
Music Makers
My Family

Community Workers

Patterns: Astronaut, page 210; Construction Worker, page 211; Crossing Guard, page 212; Doctor, page 213; Firefighter, page 214; Mail Carrier, page 215; Nurse, page 217; Police Officer, page 218; Teacher, page 219

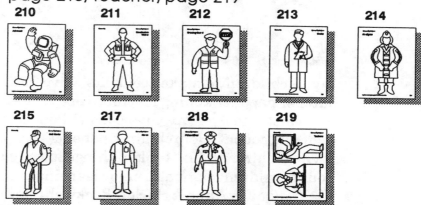

Give each child a copy of a community worker. Invite each child to color the pattern, cut it out, and glue it to one side of a 12" x 18" sheet of construction paper. Encourage children to write or dictate descriptions of the community workers' jobs on sheets of lined paper. Help children glue the descriptions beside the pictures. Children can use the descriptions to play "Who Am I?" Invite one child to read his or her description. Encourage other children to guess which community worker is being described.

Carpenter's Tool Belt

Patterns: Hammer, page 286; Wrench and Pliers, page 288;
Screwdriver, page 289

Invite children to make tool belts. Give each child a 3"-wide strip of
butcher paper or adding machine tape long enough to go around his or
her waist and overlap. Give each child a copy of the tool patterns to
color and cut out. Help children paper clip the tools to their paper belts.
Invite children to "fix" broken things in the classroom using the tools.
Young children might also enjoy learning about other tools in the book
The Toolbox by Anne & Harlow Rockwell (New York: Macmillan, 1971).

Tools of the Trade

Patterns: Astronaut, page 210; Construction Worker, page 211;
Crossing Guard, page 212; Doctor, page 213; Firefighter, page
214; Mail Carrier, page 215; Nurse, page 217; Police Officer,
page 218; Teacher, page 219

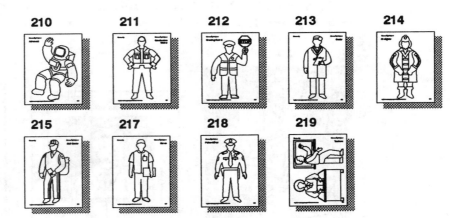

Community workers often use special tools to accomplish their jobs.
Just as a carpenter uses a hammer and nails, so a doctor, police officer,
and firefighter uses tools, too. Color, cut out, and glue each community
worker pattern to a separate piece of posterboard. Invite children to
draw or cut pictures from magazines of tools these workers might use.
Encourage children to glue the tools to the correct posterboard.

Career Displays

Patterns: Astronaut, page 210; Construction Worker, page 211; Crossing Guard, page 212; Doctor, page 213; Firefighter, page 214; Mail Carrier, page 215; Nurse, page 217; Police Officer, page 218; Teacher, page 219

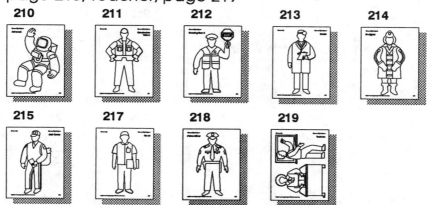

Give each child a worker pattern. Invite students to use the patterns to make posters highlighting the skills necessary for the jobs each pattern features. For example, to be a firefighter, you should be able to work calmly under dangerous conditions, understand fire safety rules, and know how to extinguish a fire. Encourage the children to be imaginative as they create the career displays.

World of Work

Patterns: Astronaut, page 210; Construction Worker, page 211; Crossing Guard, page 212; Doctor, page 213; Firefighter, page 214; Mail Carrier, page 215; Nurse, page 217; Police Officer, page 218; Teacher, page 219

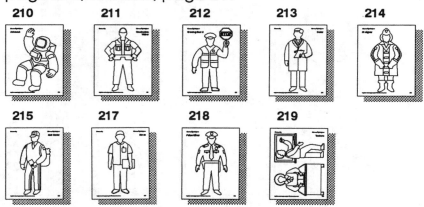

Give each child a worker pattern or invite children to draw patterns of their own. Challenge students to look in the phone book yellow pages or newspaper want ads to find a list of businesses that would hire their workers.

Sports Stars

Patterns: Ice Skate, page 13; Roller Skate, page 202; Football and Baseball, page 294; Baseball Bat and Soccer Ball, page 295; Basketball, page 296; Tennis Racket and Ball, page 293

13   **202**    **294** 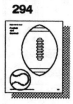   **295**   **296**   **293**

Invite students to select a pattern that represents a sport or activity they enjoy. Encourage children to make the pattern three-dimensional by placing two patterns together with stuffing in between. Children can color the patterns and staple the edges together. Invite students to imagine themselves as a professional in their chosen sport. Encourage students to write or dictate short paragraphs about their most memorable days as these famous sports figures. Display the 3-D sports items and cards on a bulletin board entitled, "Sports Heroes of Tomorrow."

People of the Past

Patterns: Christopher Columbus, page 27; Martin Luther King, Jr., page 68; Abraham Lincoln, page 70; George Washington, page 76

27    **68**    **70**    **76**

Discuss some of the important events and accomplishments in the lives of these famous people of the past. Ask four volunteers to come to the front of the room. Show the class one of the patterns without letting the volunteers see it. Tape or pin the pattern to the back of one of the volunteers. Repeat with the other three pictures until all four volunteers are facing their classmates with a famous person from the past pinned to their backs. Encourage volunteers to ask their classmates questions that require only a yes or no answer to try to discover whose picture is on their backs.

Music Makers

Patterns: Musical Instruments, pages 274-283

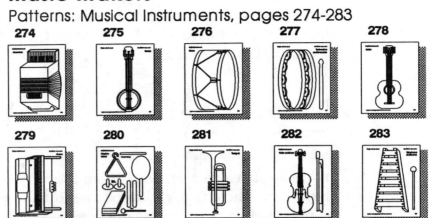

Discuss various musicians, singers, and composers, such as Stevie Wonder, Louis Armstrong, Dolly Parton, Beethoven, and Chopin. Invite students to share their own musical talents with the class and discuss their favorite musical artists. Invite students to choose their favorite instrument from the musical patterns. Encourage children to color and cut out the patterns. Challenge the children to think of a way to make a sound that might be similar to the sound of the instrument. For example, a child could imitate xylophone sounds using a spoon to tap glasses filled with different amounts of water. A student could play the drums by beating on the bottom of an empty oatmeal container. Encourage creativity.

My Family

Patterns: Apartment, page 220; Two-Story House, page 225; One-Story House, page 228

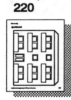  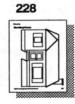

Invite the children to choose a house pattern or draw patterns of their own. Encourage children to color, cut out the pattern, and glue it to a sheet of construction paper. Invite each child to draw the members of his or her family beside the appropriate pattern. Encourage children to share their pictures with the class as they introduce their family members. (Be sensitive to a variety of family structures.)

Places

State Silhouettes
Around the World
Color-Coding Cartographers
Giant Geography
Collage Maps
U.S. Tour
School, Home, Government

State Silhouettes

Pattern: Map of the States, page 316

316

Enlarge the map of the United States on a large bulletin board. Write each state's name in the appropriate spot. Using an overhead projector, make individual state silhouettes from black construction paper. Hold up each silhouette and challenge students to identify the state by name. Encourage children to refer to the large bulletin-board map for help.

Around the World

Pattern: Globe, page 319

319

Divide the class into small cooperative groups of three or four. Give each group a copy of the globe pattern. Invite children to color the pattern, cut it out, and glue it in the center of a large sheet of construction paper or posterboard. Invite each group to choose a theme, such as clothing, food, or music, to make a multicultural poster. Read *Hats, Hats, Hats* or *Bread, Bread, Bread* by Ann Morris (New York: Lothrop, Lee & Shepard, 1989) to your students. Both of these books provide a photographic view of a theme from a worldwide perspective. Encourage the children to find interesting multicultural information or pictures. Invite children to draw pictures around the globe to represent their findings. Have children label the pictures with the name of the country they represent. Display the multicultural posters around the classroom.

Color-Coding Cartographers
Pattern: Map of the States, page 316

316

Explain to children that *cartographer* is the name given to someone who makes maps. Give each child a copy of the United States map. Encourage children to use crayons or markers to color code the following places.

Color the state you live in red.

Color the state you were born in green.

Use purple to color the largest state on the map.

Use blue to color the smallest state on the map.

Color the thirteen original colonies yellow.

Put an orange X in every state you have visited.

Put a green star in the state you would most like to visit.

Color the state with the longest coastline brown.

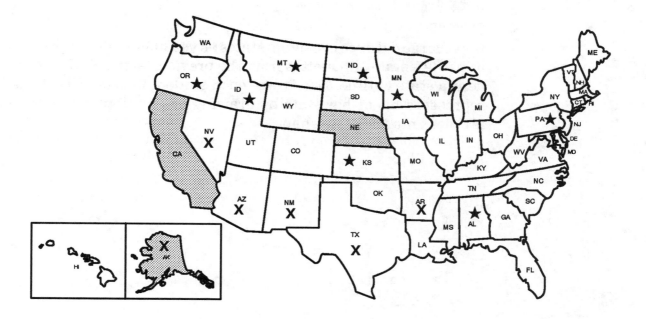

Giant Geography

Pattern: Map of the States, page 316

316

Make a large butcher paper pattern of each individual state by projecting the United States map on an overhead projector. Invite each child to trace one or two state outlines on an outdoor play surface using the large map patterns. Make sure the states fit together and then retrace the completed map on the playground with white chalk. Encourage students to use the map to play various games. Students can hop from state to state while naming the places they travel. Students can play tag on the map and designate certain states as free zones. Or, students can race each other to various locations called out by another player.

Collage Maps

Pattern: Map of the States, page 316

316

Make large outlines of enough states as you have children in your class or use the state silhouettes from the previous activity. Give each student a state outline. Encourage each student to create a collage that represents his or her state by drawing or gluing pictures and news articles onto the state shape.

U.S. Tour

Patterns: White House, page 317; Statue of Liberty, page 318;
Map of the States, page 316

317   **318**   **316**

Enlarge the United States map in the center of a bulletin board. Color
and cut out the Statue of Liberty. Mount it on a circle of construction
paper and place it on the bulletin board near the east coast. Attach a
piece of yarn from the Statue of Liberty picture to the map showing its
location in New York City. Color and cut out the White House pattern
and attach a piece of yarn to its location in Washington, DC. Discuss
the significance of these places with your students. Invite students to
draw pictures of places they have visited or would like to visit in the
United States. Add the pictures to the bulletin board and use yarn to
connect them to their locations on the map.

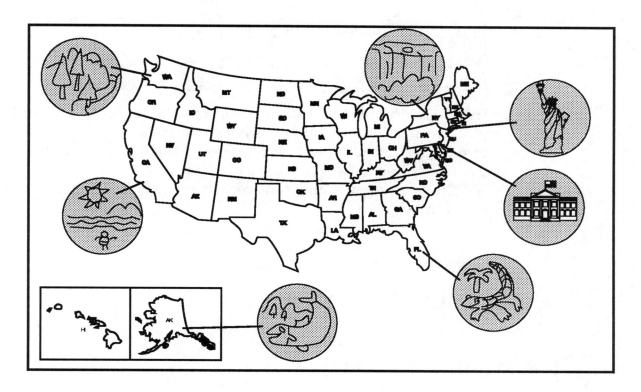

School, Home, Government

Patterns: Stop Sign, page 190; Crossing Guard, page 212; Teachers, page 219; Backpack, page 232; School, page 237; School Bus, page 238; Apartment, page 220; Bed, page 221; Lamp, page 224; Table and Chairs, page 229; Puppy, page 139; Postal Truck, page 200; Mail Carrier, page 215; Mailbox, page 216; White House, page 317; George Washington, page 76; Abraham Lincoln, page 70

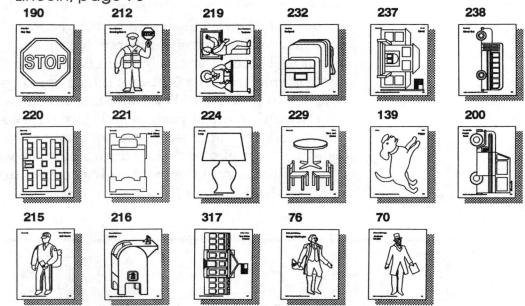

Invite children to help color and cut out the patterns. Place all the patterns in a large paper bag. Divide a large length of butcher paper into thirds. Label the sections, "School," "Home," and "Government." Invite children to take turns drawing a pattern from the bag, identifying it, and taping it under the correct category heading. Discuss the children's choices.

Transportation

Moving Along
Transportation Types
On a Roll
All Aboard
Fast or Slow, On the Go
Rules of the Road
Whirlybird
In the Driver's Seat
Floating Boats

Moving Along

Patterns: Airplane, page 192; Bicycle, page 193; Bus, page 194; Car, page 195; Fire Truck, page 196; Helicopter, page 197; Jeep, page 198; Police Car, page 199; Postal Truck, page 200; Truck, page 207

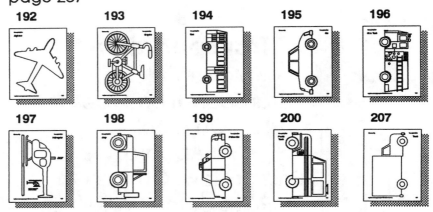

Divide the class into cooperative groups of four. Give each group a large sheet of butcher paper to create a mural showing various ways of getting from place to place. Encourage children to use paint, crayons, or markers to draw roads, bridges, airports, tunnels, and overpasses. Invite children to color and cut out patterns and glue them in place. To add insight into cultural diversity, share the book *On the Go* by Ann Morris (New York: Lothrop, Lee & Shepard, 1990). The book provides a beautiful photographic tour of various means of transportation around the world.

Transportation Types

Patterns: Transportation patterns, pages 192-209

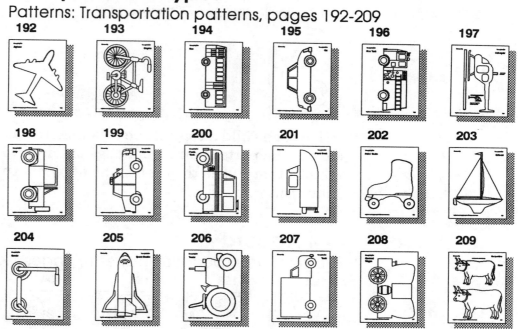

Give each student a different transportation pattern. Invite students to color and cut out the patterns. Give each child a cardboard strip. Then help the children attach the strips to the back of the patterns leaving enough room for their hands to fit underneath. Describe characteristics of the different modes of transportation. Invite each student whose pattern displays a certain characteristic to stand.

Powered by the wind

Has wheels

Powered by fuel

Flies

Can safely transport more than two people at one time

Moves faster than you can run

Can float

On a Roll
Pattern: Roller Skate, page 202

202

Give each child a copy of the roller skate pattern. Invite the children to cut the pattern out. Challenge children to make a list of as many things that roll as they can think of. Write the list on the roller skate pattern.

All Aboard
Patterns: Transportation patterns, pages 192-209

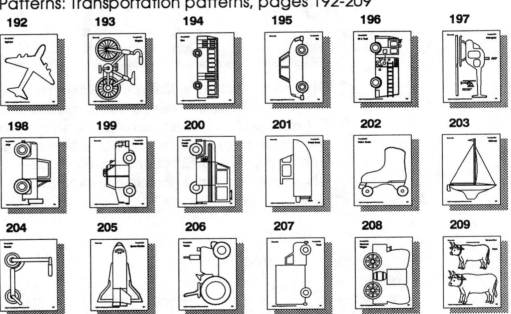

Hold up each transportation pattern one at a time. Challenge students to brainstorm a list of possible riders for each form of transportation. For example, airplane riders may include an experienced pilot, a nervous passenger, an efficient flight attendant, and a crying baby.

Fast or Slow, On the Go

Patterns: Transportation patterns, pages 192-209

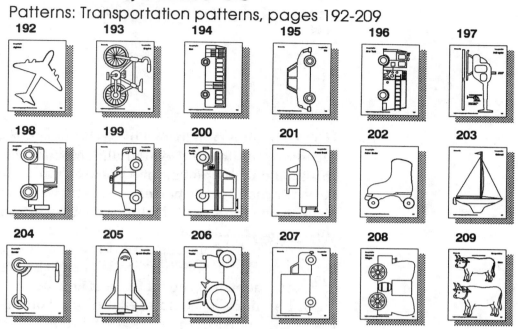

Divide the class into groups of three. Give each group three different transportation patterns. Challenge students to determine which is the fastest means of transportation and which is the slowest. As a whole class, ask each group to tell which of their vehicles is the fastest. Invite a representative from each group to hold up the pattern for all to see. Challenge the class to place the patterns in order from slowest to fastest. Repeat the exercise by asking a representative from each group to hold up the slowest means of transportation and finally the middle speed vehicle. Order these pictures by speed as well.

Rules of the Road
Pattern: Car, page 195

195

Make a simple gameboard by drawing squares in a path on a piece of tagboard. Invite children to help decorate the gameboard by drawing traffic signals, stop signs, bridges, trees, and tunnels. Reproduce several car patterns. Cut the patterns out and write a true or false driving rule on each one. Be sure to include the answer somewhere on the pattern. Cut several additional cars out and mount them on construction paper to make a deck of playing cards to go with the gameboard. A player rolls the dice and another child reads one of the driving rules. If the player correctly identifies the statement as true or false, the child can move his or her marker the number indicated on the dice. The first player to reach the end of the path is the winner.

Whirlybird

Pattern: Helicopter, page 197

197

Give each child two helicopter patterns. Invite children to cut out both patterns. Have children color the front side of one helicopter and the back side of the other. Give each child a paper cup with the bottom side up. Help children glue a helicopter to each side of the paper cup. Cut a sturdy propeller from tagboard for each child. Help children fasten the propellers to the top of the paper cups using paper fasteners.

In the Driver's Seat

Patterns: Jeep, page 198; Police Car, page 199; Power Boat, page 201; Truck, page 207; Car, page 195

198 **199** **201** **207** **195**

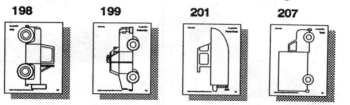

Make two enlarged copies of each pattern. Glue one pattern to each side of a box that is large enough for a child to sit in. Invite students to decorate the vehicles and create dashboards with buttons, gauges, and a steering wheel. Encourage students to role play as they sit in the driver's seat and operate the vehicles.

Floating Boats

Patterns: Power Boat, page 201; Sailboat, page 203

201   **203**

Give each child two copies of one of the boat patterns. Invite children to color the front side of one pattern and the back side of the other. Laminate the boats or cover them with clear adhesive-backed paper. Staple the open end of a quart milk carton closed for each child. Cut off one long side of each carton. The open side will be the top. Invite children to staple one of their colored boats to each side of the carton. Invite children to float the boats in a tub of water.

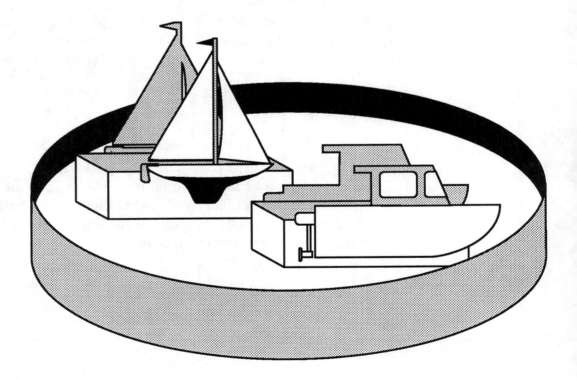

Holidays and Celebrations

Fall

Back-to-School Mobile
Bright Eyes
Trick-or-Treat Bags
Top-Notch Turkeys
Thanksgiving Scene
Fall Colors
Sunflower Mosaics
Pumpkin Patch
Columbus Day Banners

Back-to-School Mobile

Patterns: Book, page 233; Crayons, page 234; Pad and Pencil, page 235; Ruler, page 236; Scissors, page 239

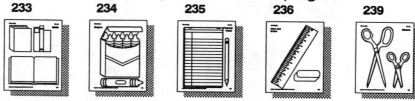

Give each student a copy of the patterns to color and cut out. Help children staple a 2"-wide construction-paper strip into a circle. Punch six holes around the circle and a hole at the top of each colored pattern. Help children tie thread through the holes and hang the back-to-school supplies at various lengths. Use thread to suspend the completed mobiles around the room.

Bright Eyes

Pattern: Jack-o'-Lantern, page 33

Give each student a jack-o'-lantern pattern that has been reproduced on orange construction paper. Invite children to cut out the pumpkin and its eyes, nose, and mouth. Encourage children to cut a green stem from construction paper and glue it in place. Help children tape or glue yellow tissue paper behind the eyes, nose, and mouth openings. Punch a hole in the top of the pumpkin and tie with a loop of yarn. Invite the children to hang "bright eyes" in a sunny window.

Trick-or-Treat Bags

Patterns: Ghost, page 30; Witch on a Broom, page 31; Jack-o'-Lantern, page 33; Black Cat, page 34; Scarecrow, page 35; Bat, page 37; Owl, page 38

Invite each child to choose one or two Halloween patterns to color and cut out. Encourage children to use the patterns to decorate trick-or-treat bags. Demonstrate other decorating ideas as well, such as fringing the top of the bag, making a handle, or adding collage materials, such as rick-rack or yarn.

Top-Notch Turkeys

Pattern: Turkey, page 46

Give each child a turkey pattern to glue on tagboard. Help the children cut the turkeys out and glue craft feathers to the tails and wings. Have children spread a thin layer of glue over the head and wattle and then sprinkle the area with red glitter. Give each child a tall triangular piece of tagboard to make a stand. Help the children make a fold down the long side of the triangle to create a thin tab. Glue the folded edge to the back of each turkey for a stand.

Thanksgiving Scene

Patterns: Pilgrim Man, page 43; Pilgrim Woman, page 44; Turkey, page 46; Indian Brave and Maiden, page 47; Place Setting, page 244; Turkey Dinner, page 246; Fish Dinner, page 247; Corn, page 5; Pumpkin, page 6; Squash, page 7; Bread, page 273

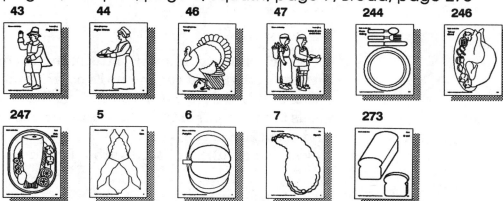

Cover a bulletin board with yellow butcher paper. Draw a long table on the paper. Enlarge patterns as necessary and trace them onto white butcher paper. Invite children to color the figures and add collage materials. Children can glue craft feathers to the turkey and scraps of fabric on the clothing. Invite children to arrange the place settings and food on the table and staple other patterns in place on the bulletin board.

Fall Colors

Patterns: Oak Leaf, page 1; Maple Leaf, page 2; Sycamore Leaf, page 3

Give each child several leaf patterns. Help the children fold the patterns in half and then unfold them. Invite children to paint one side of the leaves with tempera paint in beautiful autumn colors. Have each child fold his or her leaf pattern in half and then unfold it to make paint prints. After the leaves are dry, encourage children to cut them out. Display the leaves around the room on walls, doors, and windows.

Sunflower Mosaics

Pattern: Sunflower, page 8

Give each child a sunflower pattern. Invite children to glue the pattern on posterboard and cut it out. Encourage children to use a variety of seeds and beans to cover the flower. Students could glue sunflower seeds to the center of the flower and various colors of beans to the stem and leaves. Encourage creativity. Display the beautifully textured flowers on a bulletin board with a bright sun shining in the corner.

Pumpkin Patch

Pattern: Pumpkin, page 6

Give each student a pumpkin pattern. Invite students to color and cut out their pumpkins. Tape or staple the pumpkins along the base of your classroom walls. Connect the pumpkins with green construction-paper vines to add a fall flair to your classroom.

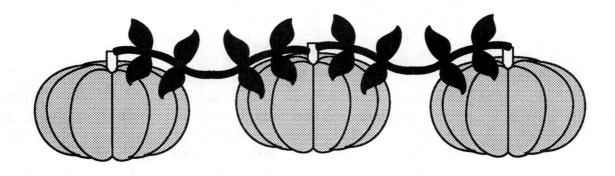

Columbus Day Banners

Patterns: Christopher Columbus, page 27; Niña, Pinta, and Santa Maria, page 29

27 **29**

Give each student a Columbus pattern and patterns for his three ships. Invite students to color and cut out the patterns. Have students glue the patterns on a vertical 12" x 18" sheet of construction paper to create a banner. Invite children to add other details using markers and crayons. Encourage children to write the names of the three ships on the banner. Help the children fringe the bottom of the banner. Then fold the top edge of the banner down one inch to make a flap. Help children string a piece of yarn under the folded edge to hang the banner.

Winter

Tissue-Paper Wreath
All the Stockings Were Hung . . .
Christmas Tree
Happy Hanukkah
Angel Choir
Christmas Bell Pot Holder
The New Year
Valentine Fingerplay
Valentine Sculpture
Valentine Tote

Tissue-Paper Wreath

Patterns: Wreath, page 52

52

Give each child a wreath pattern. Have children cut out the center circle and remove the candle. Invite children to glue the wreath on posterboard and then cut it out. Give children 1" squares of green tissue paper. Demonstrate how to wrap a tissue square around the end of a pencil, dip it in glue, and stick it to the wreath. Invite children to cover the entire wreath with tissue paper. Help the children make red crepe-paper bows to glue to the bottom of the wreaths. Attach a piece of yarn to the wreaths and invite children to hang them in the window.

All the Stockings Were Hung . . .

Pattern: Stockings, page 54

54

Read "'Twas the Night Before Christmas" to your students. Invite each child to cut several rectangular bricks from brown construction paper. Cover a bulletin board with white butcher paper. Glue or staple the bricks to the bulletin board to create a fireplace. String yarn across the top. Give each child a stocking pattern. (Use the size appropriate for your fireplace). Invite children to trace and cut two stockings from red construction paper. Staple the stockings together around the edges. Invite children to write their names in glue on their stockings. Help the children sprinkle glitter over the glue and then gently shake off the excess. Then glue cotton to the stocking cuffs and "hang" the stockings on the fireplace. Fill the stockings with small gifts, such as pencils, erasers, stickers or "I like you because . . ." notes.

Christmas Tree

Patterns: Christmas Tree, page 51; Stars, page 49; Bells, page 50; Angel, page 53; Candy Canes and Ornaments, page 55; Sled, page 10; Ice Skate, page 13; Drum, page 276; Doll, page 290; Teddy Bear, page 291; Football and Baseball, page 294; Baseball Bat, page 295; Present, page 56

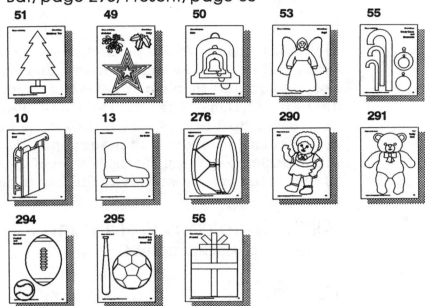

Enlarge the Christmas tree pattern and cut it out of green butcher paper. Display it on a bulletin board covered with white butcher paper. Invite children to decorate the tree using the Christmas patterns. Encourage students to make a bulletin-board border using the candy cane or star patterns. Invite children to color and cut out gifts to display around the base of the tree as well.

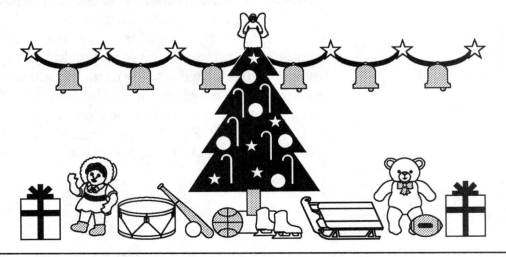

Happy Hanukkah

Pattern: Menorah, page 60

60

Lighting the menorah is an important part of the Hanukkah celebration. The candles are usually placed in the menorah from right to left. A new one is added each day. The candles are lit from left to right so the newest candle is always lit first. The candle in the center is a little bit higher than the rest. It is used to light the others. Give each child a menorah pattern. Have children cut around the menorah and glue it to a sheet of construction paper. Invite children to trace and cut nine candles and nine flames from construction paper. Have children glue a candle in each candle holder and then glue flames above the candles to "light" them.

Angel Choir

Pattern: Angel, page 53

53

Cover a bulletin board with deep blue butcher paper. Staple silver garland around the bulletin board as a border. Give each child an angel pattern to cut out. Help the children cut pieces of yarn to glue to the angel's hair. Invite children to outline the wings with glue and sprinkle with gold or silver glitter. Display the choir of angels on the bulletin board. Spread wisps of cotton along the bottom. Cut musical notes from black construction paper and staple in place among the angels.

Christmas Bell Pot Holder

Pattern: Bells, page 50

50

Give each child a bell pattern. Help each child trace and cut two bells from red or green felt. Add a layer of cotton batting between the two figures. Invite children to carefully stitch the three layers together around the edges.

The New Year

Patterns: Clock, page 65; Hat, Balloon, and Noisemaker, page 66

65   **66**

Cover a bulletin board with white butcher paper. Enlarge the clock face using an overhead projector and trace it onto the bulletin board. Color the numbers on the clock face and position both clock hands so they are pointing toward the twelve. Give each student a balloon, noisemaker, or hat pattern. Invite children to write a New Year's resolution on their patterns and then color and cut the patterns out. Display the figures and some crepe-paper streamers on a bulletin board entitled, "A New Beginning."

Valentine Fingerplay

Pattern: Hearts, page 75

75

Make several small heart patterns from tagboard. Invite each child to use a tagboard pattern to trace and cut out five red hearts from construction paper. Children can use a marker to draw faces on the hearts. Give the children small paper strips to use to make finger puppets. Help the children measure and glue the paper strips to the back of each heart in order to fit the students' fingers. Encourage children to wear a heart finger puppet on each finger as they do the following fingerplay.

One red valentine says, "I love you."

Annie made another; then there were two.

Two red valentines. One just for me.

Hosea made another; then there were three.

Three red valentines. We need one more.

Mei Li made another; then there were four.

Four red valentines. Well, sakes alive!

Carlos made another; then there were five.

Five red valentines, made just today.

"Be my valentine" is what they say.

Valentine Sculpture

Pattern: Hearts, page 75

75

Reproduce the heart pattern on red construction paper and give each child a copy. Invite children to cut around each heart on the sides, but do not cut through the top and bottom. Help the children fold each heart shape forward (except the largest one). Have children mount the largest heart on a sheet of white construction paper.

Valentine Tote

Pattern: Valentine, page 73

73

Reproduce the valentine pattern on red or pink construction paper. Give each child two patterns. Invite children to cut the hearts out. Have children place the hearts back-to-back and staple the edges leaving the top open. Encourage the children to make handles by cutting strips of red or pink paper and gluing and stapling them to each side of the open totes.

Spring and Summer

Speckled Eggs
St. Patrick's Day
In Like a Lion, Out Like a Lamb
Easter Basket
Flower Bloom Sachets
You're a Grand Old Flag
Firecracker Fun

Speckled Eggs

Pattern: Easter Egg, page 83

83

Reproduce the largest egg on a variety of colors of construction paper. Give each child one colorful egg. Invite each child to cut away the inside of the egg leaving a 1/2" frame. Have each child lay the egg frame on a sheet of waxed paper. Invite children to use table knives to make crayon shavings inside the egg frames. Place another sheet of waxed paper over the top of the crayon shavings. Iron over the egg frames with a warm iron. Have the children trim the waxed paper around the edges of the frames. Hang the speckled eggs in a sunny window.

St. Patrick's Day

Patterns: Shamrocks, page 79; Leprechaun, page 80; Rainbow, page 22; Money, page 324

79 80 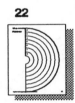 22  324

Cover a bulletin board with white butcher paper. Using an overhead projector, enlarge the rainbow on the bulletin board. Invite students to help color its arches, beginning with the outer arch (red, orange, yellow, green, blue, indigo, violet). Make a pot of gold and place it at the end of the rainbow. Reproduce the coins on yellow construction paper. Invite students to cut them out and glue or staple them in the pot. Enlarge the leprechaun and invite students to color and cut him out. Staple him next to the pot of gold. Reproduce the shamrock pattern on green construction paper and give each student a copy. Invite students to cut out the shamrocks. Place the smaller shamrocks around the border of the bulletin board. Place the larger ones where appropriate.

In Like a Lion, Out Like a Lamb

Patterns: Lion, page 110; Lamb, page 164

110   **164**

Give each child a lion and a lamb pattern to glue on tagboard. Help children cut the figures out. Invite the children to dip yellow yarn in a liquid starch and glue mixture and place it in an interesting design on the lion. Invite children to glue cotton balls to the lamb. Create a wall display using the animal creations to show the many weather moods of unpredictable March.

Easter Basket

Pattern: Easter Basket and Candy, page 81

81

Give each child a copy of the Easter basket and candy pattern. Invite children to color the basket so it looks woven. Using a crayon, demonstrate how to draw a 1" square of vertical lines, a 1" square of horizontal lines, a 1" square of vertical lines, and so on across the rows until the entire basket is colored. Have children cut the basket out. Give each child a handful of plastic grass to glue to the inside of the basket. Invite children to trace and cut out several eggs from construction paper and glue them to the grass. Children can color and cut out the candy bunnies and chicks to add to the baskets as well.

Flower Bloom Sachets

Patterns: Daisy, page 16; Tulip, page 17; Rose, page 19

16 **17**  **19**

Reproduce the flower patterns on white construction paper and give two patterns of the same flower to each student. Invite children to cut around the patterns and color them. Remind children to color the front side of one pattern and the back side of the other. Help each child place a piece of cotton saturated with perfume or after-shave lotion between the flower blossoms to make a sachet. Invite children to glue the two flowers together around the edges. Punch two pinholes in the sachet. Try substituting flower petal potpourri or kitchen spices and extracts for the perfume. Encourage the children to give the sachets to someone they love for a special occasion.

You're a Grand Old Flag

Pattern: American Flag, page 87

87

In celebration of Flag Day, invite children to trace the American flag pattern onto thin white fabric. Pin the pattern underneath the fabric to hold it in place while children trace. Invite children to use fabric crayons or markers to color alternating stripes red, starting at the top. Have children color the square blue. Supervise children as they use a needle and thread to make small cross stitches with white embroidery thread (for stars) in the blue square. Help the children wrap the end of the flag with the stars around a dowel and glue in place.

Firecracker Fun

Pattern: Firecracker, page 89

89

Give each child an empty toilet-paper tube. Invite children to paint the tubes with red, white, and blue tempera paint. Give each child a copy of the firecracker pattern. While the tubes are drying, invite the children to color and cut out the explosion sections of the patterns. Invite children to glue the patterns to the fronts of their firecracker tubes. Fill each child's firecracker with peanuts in the shell. Encourage children to lift the tubes off their desks and watch the explosion as the peanuts fall out. Invite children to enjoy their treats.

Self-Esteem Celebrations
Birthday Celebrations
Piñata Party
Showers of Praise
Sunshine Spotlight
I'm Someone Special
Something to Spout About

Birthday Celebrations

Patterns: Cake with Candle, page 67; Hat, Balloon, and Noise-maker, page 66

67   **66**

Enlarge the birthday cake, decorate, and cut it out. Place the birthday cake in the center of a bulletin board covered with colorful background paper. Give each student a copy of the hat, balloon, and noisemaker pattern. Invite children to color and cut out the patterns. Use the patterns to make a festive border around the bulletin board. Enlarge the candle pattern and reproduce one copy for each child. Invite children to color and cut out their candles. Write each child's name and birth date on his or her candle. Add each child's candle to the cake on his or her special day.

Piñata Party

Pattern: Piñata, page 62

62

Read *Hello, Amigos!* by Tricia Brown (New York: Holt, 1986) to your students. In the story, it's Frankie Valdez's special day—his birthday. At his birthday party, he has a mariachi band, some of his favorite foods, and a piñata. Help students become aware that children celebrate birthdays in many different ways all over the world. Invite children to share some of their favorite ways to celebrate their special day. Then share in Frankie's fun by making mini-piñatas. Give each student two copies of the piñata pattern. Invite students to color the patterns and cut them out. Remind students to color the front side of one pattern and the back side of the other. Give each student a piece of candy to place between the patterns. Help children staple around the edges. Punch a hole in the top of the patterns. Invite children to string yarn through the holes so they can hang their piñatas.

Showers of Praise

Pattern: Umbrella, page 321

321

Enlarge the umbrella pattern and display it on a good work bulletin board entitled, "Showers of Praise." Make large raindrops from blue construction paper and place them at random on the bulletin board. Display student work by stapling papers to the raindrops. Acknowledge children's abilities and praise their efforts.

Sunshine Spotlight

Pattern: Sun, page 25

25

Assign each child a special week out of the year when he or she is spotlighted. Invite children to bring special photos or other items from home that tell something about themselves. Reproduce the sun pattern on yellow or orange construction paper. Cut the pattern out and place it in the corner of a posterboard. Title the poster, "The Sun Is Shining on (child's name)." Display photos or other items the child brings from home on the poster. Invite the child to tell about the items on display. Give the child the poster to take home at the end of the week.

I'm Someone Special

Pattern: Face, page 240

240

Give each student a face pattern. Invite children to color and cut out the faces and glue them on construction paper. Encourage children to color and cut out facial features to make face pictures that are uniquely theirs. Encourage each child to cut and glue yarn the appropriate color and length of his or her own hair onto the face pattern. Remind students that we all have special and unique features, talents, and abilities. Display the finished faces on a bulletin board entitled, "I'm Someone Special."

Something to Spout About

Pattern: Blue Whale, page 141

141

Prepare a good work bulletin board to highlight student achievements. Cover the board with white butcher paper. Enlarge the whale and water spout pattern and cut them from blue construction paper. Place the whale in the center of the board. Staple 8 1/2" x 11" sheets of construction paper on both sides of the whale. Pin examples of student work to the blue paper. Cut black letters from construction paper to title the board, "Something to Spout About."

Index